AGNES K. MISSIRIAN holds a Ph.D. from the University of Massachusetts and is Associate Professor of Strategic Management at Bentley College, Waltham, Massachusetts. A former director of communications, she is a seasoned public speaker, the author of numerous articles in professional journals, and a program developer for both the private and public sectors.

Agnes K. Missirian, Ph.D.

The Corporate Connection

WHY EXECUTIVE WOMEN NEED MENTORS TO REACH THE TOP

COLLEGE FOR HUMAN SERVICES
LIBRARY
345 HUDSON STREET
NEW YORK, N.Y. 10014

A SPECTRUM BOOK

Prentice-Hall, Inc. Englewood Cliffs, New Jersey 07632

Library of Congress Cataloging in Publication Data

Missirian, Agnes K.
   The corporate connection.

"A Spectrum Book."
Bibliography: p.
Includes index.
   1. Women executives.   2. Women in business.   3. Success.   I. Title.
HF5500.2.M515   658.4'09'088042   81-22709
                                        AACR2

ISBN 0-13-173187-4 {PBK}

ISBN 0-13-173195-5

This Spectrum Book is available to businesses and organizations at a special discount when ordered in large quantities. For information, contact Prentice-Hall, Inc., General Book Division, Special Sales, Englewood Cliffs, N. J. 07632.

© 1982 by Agnes K. Missirian

A SPECTRUM BOOK

All rights reserved. No part of this book may be reproduced in any form or by any means without permission in writing from the author and the publisher.

1   2   3   4   5   6   7   8   9   10

Printed in the United States of America

Editorial/production supervision by Cyndy Lyle Rymer
Manufacturing buyer: Cathie Lenard

Prentice-Hall International, Inc., *London*
Prentice-Hall of Australia Pty. Limited, *Sydney*
Prentice-Hall of Canada, Ltd., *Toronto*
Prentice-Hall of India Private Limited, *New Delhi*
Prentice-Hall of Japan, Inc., *Tokyo*
Prentice-Hall of Southeast Asia Pte. Ltd., *Singapore*
Whitehall Books Limited, *Wellington, New Zealand*

To my mother,
who inspired me to strive for the best in myself
and to look for the best in others.

Contents

Preface, ix

chapter one
Mentoring as a phenomenon, 1

chapter two
The elusive corporate woman, 9

chapter three
100 top businesswomen: a unique population, 21

chapter four
The protégés, 33

chapter five
The pygmalion syndrome: initiation, 39

chapter six
Total commitment: development, 50

chapter seven
Infinite closeness: termination, 63

chapter eight
Mentoring relationships gone awry, 73

chapter nine
**Agapē versus sex
in mentoring relationships**, 80

chapter ten
**An analysis
for the mentoring phenomenon**, 85

chapter eleven
**What to do 'til
the mentor comes**, 97

Bibliography, 110

Index, 115

Preface

> A great society is a society in which its men of business think greatly of their functions.
>
> ALFRED NORTH WHITEHEAD

The foregoing quotation crystallizes the concept of business espoused by my mentors. It is this broad, philosophical view of business that is their legacy to me. Were Whitehead writing today, I am certain he would have said: "A great society is a society in which its men *and women* of business think greatly of their functions." In any case, that is how I interpret his thoughts.

Because of the growing number of women entering management ranks today, there is a vital need to examine the policies and practices instrumental in developing women into effective and successful managers.

Review of the literature indicates that the mentor/protégé relationship is a key element in the career patterns of successful male managers. The literature is silent about the prevalence or effect of mentoring on female managers.

This study examines the prevalence and the process of mentoring experienced by a select group of woman managers. A sample was drawn from women at the top of the organizational hierarchy—women who are active, practicing managers; women who are neither entrepreneurs nor heiresses; women who made their way to the top through the corporate hierarchy.

The investigation was exploratory in nature, consisting of a survey of the one hundred top businesswomen in the country together with fifteen in-depth interviews. The general hypothesis—that mentoring has been a significant part of the career development of successful female managers—was confirmed.

The following research questions were also explored:

- Is the mentor/protégé relationship as described by Daniel J. Levinson different as it applies to female managers?
- Are there stages of socialization or patterns of behavior within the mentor/protégé relationship that can be clearly identified?
- Do mentors and their protégés have shared values, attitudes, and goals?
- Are mentors former protégés?
- Is the issue of voluntary association important? The issue of initiation?
- Is sexuality addressed in the mentor/protégé relationship?

For each question the data support an affirmative answer.

The principal outcome of this research is the description of the mentoring process. Three broad phases—Initiation, Development, and Termination—are described in detail. A set of mentor behaviors is specified together with correlative sets of perceptions and feelings experienced by protégés during each phase of the mentoring process. Analysis of the data reveals that although it is the mentor who initiates the process, it is the protégé who signals the shift from one stage to the next.

This research also reveals three characteristic elements that distinguish mentoring relationships (the highest point on a continuum of supportive relationships) from other less influential relationships: (1) the degree of power the mentor commands in terms of access to resources, both material and personal; (2) the level of identification with the mentor; and (3) the intensity of emotional involvement with the mentor.

Although mentoring relationships are unique, complex, and relatively rare in the organizational context, this study presents evidence to support the view that this powerful ideal can be approximated, if not fully reached, at all levels of the organization.

The following chapters elaborate on the foregoing in considerable detail, and the final chapter offers a pragmatic prescription for career success. What is not addressed in the text is my motivation for pursuing this research. In retrospect I realize that it was prompted by a personal desire to understand the complexity of my own experiences as a protégé.

My first mentor, Maurice Simon, was a prominent Boston attorney. He was a powerful man—brilliant, dynamic, incisive, and caring. He was a moral man, a gentleman, with qualities of character rare at any time and in any profession. He was the protégé of Homer Albers, distinguished dean of the Boston University Law School.

As a young woman of 18 fresh out of Katharine Gibbs, I became the fortunate beneficiary of Simon's attention and tutelage. Without casting aspersions on any of the fine men and women with whom I have worked and studied these past years, I have *never* learned more about the conduct of business, finance, and the law than I did as his secretary. I learned by listening. I learned by doing. I learned by his example. The opportunity to learn was never denied me. It is significant that the gift he gave me to mark my twenty-first birthday was his power of attorney. It was my rite of passage.

In the ensuing years, I pursued a business career of my own that he followed with pride and pleasure. It is a source of considerable pain to me that he did not live long enough to know that it was our long and loving relationship that prompted the research for which I received my doctoral hood.

My second mentor and dear friend is Harry Levinson, distinguished professor, author, and consultant. While pursuing my MBA, I had the good fortune to study human behavior with him. He has the ability, rare among teachers, to inspire his students with his teaching and his persona.

Harry Levinson is also clairvoyant. When I consulted him about the wisdom of pursuing an academic career, he charted a course for me that predicted every obstacle an outspoken, independent businesswoman could possibly encounter in Academe. And yes, I hit every single one of them! Significantly, he was the first academic to treat me as a colleague, a fact that says much more about him than it does about me. Inevitably, much of my thinking and my behavior as a teacher are rooted in what I have learned from him.

The body of knowledge about mentoring in complex organizations is still relatively limited. Without question, as the importance of supportive relations in organizational life for both men and women is more widely recognized, there will be an increase in the research on mentoring and other supportive relationships. The overall pattern of the process of mentoring described here will be enriched and refined by such research.

As our knowledge of these powerful relationships increases, it is hoped that our understanding will contribute to the enrichment and quality of organizational life.

Acknowledgments

Many people contributed to the preparation of this volume from its beginning as a dissertation through its transformation into a book. I should like to express my sincere appreciation and gratitude to each where that is possible.

The most important contribution came from the distinguished businesswomen who participated in this study. Without their cooperation, candor, and considerable generosity of time, this study would not have been possible. I took particular care during the preparation of the book to preserve their anonymity, so that naming them now, even to express my gratitude, would violate a promise of confidentiality.

Special thanks are extended to the faculty of the University of Massachusetts at Amherst, particularly the members of my dissertation committee: Joseph A. Litterer, committee chairman, not only for his guidance and constructive criticism, but also for his patience, sensitivity, and support throughout the research process and beyond; D. Anthony Butterfield for his thoughtful comments and encouragement; Arthur Elkins for all his assistance and enthusiastic support; and Alice S. Rossi for her consistent interest and valuable critiques. To Donald Frederick,

George Odiorne, Sidney Sufrin, and Max Wortman also, my special thanks are extended for their unique contribution to my work and to my professional growth.

A debt of gratitude is acknowledged to the National Business and Professional Women's Foundation for awarding me a fellowship that helped to finance this research.

A special note of thanks to my friend and colleague, Arie Reichel, who offered his good counsel and companionship; to my dear friend Cynthia Citron, who was always ready with a sympathetic ear, valuable insights, and much encouragement; and to my good friend Edward Mattar, who directed me in the difficult process of transforming an academic dissertation into a publishable book. Special thanks also to Mary Daly, who supervised the typing of the manuscript, and to Denise LaBrache and Micki Tidd, who deciphered my frightful handwriting with good humor.

Most of all I wish to acknowledge the continuous support, tolerance, and love I received from my family. Without their encouragement I probably would not have started this work, and I surely would not have been able to finish it.

chapter one

Mentoring as a phenomenon

> Treat people as if they were what they ought to be and you help them to become what they are capable of being.
> GOETHE

Remember the Greek legend of Pygmalion, the sculptor who fell in love with his creation Galatea? How about their modern counterparts, Liza and the indefatigable Henry Higgins, the professor who transformed the marble-mouthed flower girl into an elegant duchess?

These charming stories capture our imagination and excite our romantic fantasies. But on closer examination they underscore one of the more fundamental aspects of human relationships: the influence of one person's expectations on another's behavior.

More than half a century ago, Albert Moll concluded from his clinical experience that subjects behaved as they believed they were expected to. "The prophecy causes its own fulfillment," he observed. And in a series of scientific experiments, Rosenthal demonstrated that a "teacher's expectations for her pupils' intellectual competence can come to serve as an educational self-fulfilling prophecy."

Certainly managerial behavior is not exempt from this phenomenon. The manager has the potential not only to shape the expectations and productivity of his or her subordinates but also to influence their attitudes toward their jobs and themselves.

BREAKING INTO THE "IN" GROUP

Who is it who performs this critical role in preparing aspiring young managers for membership in the organization's elite corps?

If you were to ask any one of the Young Turks (alternatively referred to as organizational "comers," "fast-trackers," "fair-haired boys," or "water-walkers") what it takes to break into top management, he would undoubtedly answer: a mentor, a sponsor...a "godfather." Indeed, the notion that an aspiring young manager needs a mentor or a sponsor to advance to the highest levels of the corporate hierarchy has such a degree of face validity that very little empirical research exists regarding this phenomenon in the corporate context.

What little research there is supports the popular notion. Access to the upper echelons of many of the traditional professions—law, medicine, theology, higher education, and more recently, management—is commonly gained through the protégé and/or colleague system. Both operate to identify, train, and groom the neophytes who will become the future leaders of the profession. The interplay between the formal and informal relationships of the practitioners in these professions is a significant part of the socialization and developmental process.

The close rapport that results from working together, dining together, playing together, relaxing together makes it possible for the developing young person not only to acquire expertise in the technical and functional aspects of the work itself, but also to internalize those values and to develop those work habits, interpersonal skills, and mannerisms that distinguish the members of the profession. Ultimately, these carefully cultivated characteristics will identify the neophyte as sufficiently competent and personally "worthy" to be admitted into the inner circle of the professional community.

If one wants to become a top manager, then, how important is it to be a member of the "in" group? What does one have to do? Who does one have to know to get one's foot in the door? A quick look at some earlier research findings might provide some clues—even some tentative answers.

(For anyone who wants to read these sources in greater detail, references are provided in the bibliography.)

Becker and Strauss (1956) observe that one has to be regarded as "in" even to learn the job itself, and that "until the newcomer is accepted, he will not be taught crucial trade secrets," much less advance in the field. Stressing the subtleties of the informal relationships, Goffman (1963) points out that "more is involved than norms regarding somewhat static status attributes...that failure to sustain the many minor norms important in the etiquette of face-to-face communications can have a very pervasive effect upon the defaulter's acceptability in social situations." The work of Hall (1948) illustrates these same points for the medical profession, and the work of Egerton (cited in Bernard, 1964) for the sciences.

In the specific case of management, Zaleznik (1977) goes a step further and draws a distinction between managers as professionals and as leaders of the profession. He suggest that whereas low and middle managers are socialized by the organizational norms, the most promising young managers—those destined to become top managers and leaders of the profession—are socialized on a one-to-one basis by a mentor or a sponsor.

Some business firms have recognized the importance of mentoring in developing managers. Jewel Companies, for example, has had an institutionalized form of mentoring for junior executives for some time based on former chairman Frank Lunding's belief in its effectiveness as a developmental strategy. In his book, *Sharing a Business,* he calls it the "first assistant" philosophy. Significantly, each of the last four presidents of Jewel was the mentor of his successor. Two other firms, AT&T and RCA, have started experimenting with peer-group mentoring programs designed for women and minorities entering the management ranks.

Given the appropriate educational background, the professional expertise and the requisite motivation, then, it appears that one of the critical developmental factors in the socialization of the most successful managers is the degree of sophistication and acceptance gained through personal rapport with a member or members of the professional elite.

The Mentoring of Men

A survey conducted by Heidrick & Struggles, Inc., published in the *Harvard Business Review* (January/February, 1979), reports that top managers not only have had mentors but apparently derive greater satisfaction from their career and work than those do who have not had mentors. Nearly two-thirds of the respondents reported having had a mentor or a sponsor, and one-third of them have had two or more mentors. (It is noteworthy that of the 1250 respondents, less than 1 percent were women.) The survey suggests further that executives who have had a mentor earn more money at a younger age, are better educated, are more likely to follow a career plan, and sponsor more protégés than executives who have not had a mentor.

Some writers in the management literature, notably Berlew and Hall, Etzioni, Livingston, Schein, Zaleznik and others, have reported on the corporate socialization process and tangentially on elements of the mentor/protégé relationship. The most extensive investigations of mentoring to date are those of Daniel J. Levinson (1978), Harry Levinson (1968), and Shapiro, Haseltine, and Rowe (1978).

In his study of adult male development, Daniel J. Levinson cites the role of mentor as critical in the fulfillment of a young man's "dream" (ego ideal) in terms of both professional and emotional development. He points out that the absence of a mentor is associated with "various kinds of developmental impairment and problems of individuation in mid-life." He reported on the life cycle of 40 men: 10 blue- and white-collar workers in industry; 10 academicians; 10 biologists and novelists; and 10 business executives.

Following is a summary of Levinson's description of the mentor and the formation of mentoring relationships:

> A good mentor is an admixture of good father and good friend. (A bad mentor, of which there are many, combines the worst features of father and friend.) A "good enough" mentor is a transitional figure who invites and welcomes a young man into the adult world. He serves as guide, teacher and sponsor. He represents skill, knowledge, virtue, accomplishment—the superior qualities a young man hopes someday to acquire. He gives his blessing to the novice and his dream. And yet, with all this superiority, he conveys the promise that in time, they will be peers. The protégé has the hope that soon he will be able to join or even surpass his mentor in the work they both value.

> A mentor can be of great practical help to a young man as he seeks to find his way and gain new skills. But a good mentor is helpful in a more basic, developmental sense. The relationship enables the recipient to identify with a person who exemplifies many of the quali-

ties he seeks. It enables him to form an internal figure who offers love, admiration and encouragement in his struggles. He acquires a sense of belonging to the generation of promising young men. He reaps the various benefits to be gained from a serious, mutual non-sexual loving relationship with a somewhat older man or woman. (There are other elements, which bring various advantages and disadvantages when the relationship is sexual and when the mentor is much older or the same age.)

Like all love relationships, the course of a mentor relationship is rarely smooth and its ending is often painful. Such relations have favorable developmental functions, but they have negative aspects as well. There is plenty of room for exploitation, undercutting, envy, smothering and oppressive control on the part of the mentor, and for greedy demanding clinging admiration, self-denying gratitude and arrogant ingratitude on the part of the recipient. It is not always clear who is doing what for whom. After the relationship has been terminated, both parties are susceptible to the most intense feelings of admiration and contempt, appreciation and resentment, grief, rage, bitterness, and relief—just as in the wake of any significant love relationship.

Daniel J. Levinson concludes that most adults give and receive very little mentoring; that despite the frequent emphasis on teamwork and loyalty in business organizations, mentoring relationships are more the exception than the rule for both workers and managers.

The foregoing description of the mentor appears in an earlier theoretical and psychological conception by Harry Levinson, entitled *The Exceptional Executive*. He describes the mentoring relationship in terms of meeting the ministration, maturation and mastery needs of subordinates and/or protégés. He also emphasizes the importance of "giving one's blessing" to the protégé's aspirations in the ministration stage and "letting go" in the mastery stage. In return, the younger person feels appreciation, admiration, respect, gratitude, love and identification. In some respects the main value of the relationship is created after it ends, says Levinson. "The protégé's personality is enriched as he makes the valued qualities of the mentor more fully a part of himself."

Shapiro, Haseltine and Rowe describe a range of advisory/guiding persons, often called "mentors," who facilitate access to positions of leadership, authority or power for their respective protégés. Such people, they say, form a continuum with "mentors" and "peer pals" as end points.

They perceive the "mentor" as the most intense and paternalistic of the type of patron described by the continuum. These are the so-called "godfathers" and "rabbis" to which Kanter, Sheehy and other writers have referred. "Sponsors" serve as a two-thirds point on the continuum. While strong supporters, they are less powerful than mentors in promoting and shaping the careers of their protégés. The one-third, or "guide" role, is filled by those who are less able than mentors and sponsors to fulfill the roles of benefactor, protector or champion to their protégés. However, they can be invaluable in explaining the system, pointing out pitfalls to be avoided and shortcuts to be pursued. And finally, they identify "peer pals" who clearly cannot be godfathers to one another, but who can share information and advice and act as sounding boards for one another.

Shapiro et al suggest further that those relationships that fall toward the "mentor" side of the continuum tend to be more hierarchical and parental, more intense and exclusionary, and therefore more elitist. Those relationships which fall toward the "peer pal" side of the continuum tend to be more egalitarian, less intense and exclusionary.

The Mentoring of Women

If we assume, then, that the "mentor"—however defined—is a critical developmental figure in the life cycle of men, and if we assume further that membership in the professional elite is best mediated by a mentor, it seems reasonable to hypothesize that the mentor can also be a critical developmental figure in the life cycle of female managers.

Various authors—Epstein (1969), Hennig (1971), Sheehy (1976), and Kanter (1977)—have alluded to the importance of a mentor, trusted counselor, sponsor, coach, guide, etc., in the career patterns of women. However, the mentor/protégé relationship was not the primary focus of their research, nor was there any consistency in their definition of a professional, an executive or a managerial woman.

Epstein (1969) observes that, because their sex status is defined within the culture of the traditional professions as inappropriate, women find that institutionalized channels of recruitment and advancement such as the protégé system are not available to them. While this is an enlightening conclusion, it would be unwise to extrapolate from the traditional professions directly into the corporate context. The organizational structure in which the traditional professionals operate is significantly different from most corporate structures in which managers operate.

Hennig (1971) identified a sponsor as a significant figure in the career development of the women executives she interviewed, but the principal sponsor in most cases was the woman's father, who provided access into the organizational hierarchy. While this finding is psychologically intriguing, it would be hard to generalize to the larger population of organization women today, whose fathers may be neither business executives nor professionals with clout.

Using an historical perspective, Sheehy (1977) examines the sometimes notorious lives of celebrated women in the arts who were the protégés of famous men. In most cases the mentor was either husband or lover. Again, Sheehy's sample can hardly be considered representative. Moreover, she readily acknowledges that her analysis of the mentor relationship is drawn directly from Daniel J. Levinson's research.

The most recent study on mentoring for female managers is a dissertation by Linda Lee Phillips entitled "Mentors and Protégés: A Study of the Career Development of Women Managers and Executives in Business and Industry" (UCLA, School of Education, 1977).

While exploring the totality of the stages in women's careers, the study focused upon "the concept of 'career mentoring'—the help given by someone (mentor) to an individual (protégé) in order to help the protégé define or reach his or her life goals." Sixty-one percent of the women stated that they had one or more career mentors during their lifetimes. Phillips identified "primary" and "secondary" mentors. Primary mentors, according to Phillips, are those who "go out on a limb" for their protégés and really care. Secondary mentors, though also helpful, are essentially out to benefit themselves rather than the protégé. "The difference between primary and secondary mentors," she concludes, "depends entirely upon the perception of the protégé not the perceptions of the mentors or outside observers." She also concludes that most mentor/protégé relationships go through a series of phases, which she calls Initiation, Sparkle, Development, Disillusionment, Parting and Transformation.

She outlines three dimensions which contribute to the success or failure of the mentoring experience: *"the mentoring relationship* (the participants' attitudes toward themselves, each other, and the experience, their needs and personal characteristics, the length of the relationship, and the participants' reasons for and control over participating), *the mentoring help* (appropriateness and potential impact), and *the timing* of the experience (when it occurs within each participant's career stages and within the external environment)." Each of these must be present, she says, for the effect of the relationship to be a positive one for both mentor and protege.

The sample was drawn from *Standard and Poor's Register of Corporations, Directors and Executives* and *Who's Who In Finance & Industry* plus the 100 women named by *Business Week* as the "100 Top Corporate Women."

While the study adds to our understanding of mentoring in general, it deals with an essentially heterogeneous sample. Many of the women included in the *Standard and Poor's Register* and *Who's Who in Finance* are not practicing managers but corporate directors who may not have a business or corporate orientation at all. They may be economists, attorneys, Ph.D.'s or the wives or daughters of majority shareholders—though not necessarily managers.

A host of other authors writing in both professional and popular journals have emphasized: (1) the importance of a sponsor or mentor as a means of "getting to the top" or advancing professionally; (2) the dearth of female mentors to serve as counselors and role models for female managers; (3) the sexual overtones surrounding male/female mentor/protégé relationships. and (4) speculation as to how these factors may influence the advancement of women in organizations. However, these articles are not empirically based for the most part and appear to be infinite variations or distortions of the research findings cited here.

What can we say then about mentoring as a phenomenon? For a start we might conclude that most successful male managers and many successful female managers have had a mentor or a sponsor, and that in general, mentoring is regarded as a positive phenomenon. However, very little is known about the process of mentoring for either group from which one could generalize. And to obfuscate what little is known, the term "mentoring" has been used to describe a wide range of behaviors characterized by varying degrees of emotional involvement and intensity.

In view of this scarcity of empirical data concerning the process of mentoring, it was our intent to examine the prevalence and the process of mentoring in a homogeneous and select group of women at the very top of the organizational hierarchy—women who are active, practicing managers; women who are neither entrepreneurs nor heiresses; women who made their way to the top through the corporate maze.

chapter two

The elusive corporate woman

> I would venture to guess that Anon., who wrote so many poems without signing them, was often a woman.
> VIRGINIA WOOLF

As John Kenneth Galbraith pointed out in *The Affluent Society,* conventional ideas become most vulnerable when the march of events makes them outdated and irrelevant. Ever since World War II the *reality* of women's "place" has ceased to conform to the stereotype.

WOMEN IN MANAGEMENT: A POST-WORLD WAR II PHENOMENON

In the overall history of women and work in America, World War II stands as the most decisive breaking point. The eruption of hostilities generated an unprecedented demand for new workers and new production. Almost overnight female employment became a national necessity instead of a social aberration. Over two million women went to work in offices during the war, half of them for Uncle Sam. Not surprisingly, women workers found that they enjoyed their jobs, that they welcomed the opportunity to associate with others in the office or on the assembly line, and that they valued the paycheck which was their reward.

Perhaps most significant, the women who took jobs in the years after the war tended increasingly to come from the middle class. The war itself, of course, legitimized employment for people of all social and economic backgrounds. In addition, the rapid growth of clerical work and white-collar occupations created positions which were not inconsistent with middle-class status. The continued growth of the white-collar sector of the economy coincided with the rapid increase of employment among middle-class women.

Rising aspirations, infectious consumerism, the desire to send their children to a good college, and the spiral of inflation all did their part to make the continued employment of middle-class women a necessity for living "the good life" in America.

As a result of all these forces, the shape of the female labor force was drastically altered. To be sure, the vast majority of women continue to work in sex-segregated occupations, concentrating in service industries, clerical jobs, government positions, manufacturing, teaching, and nursing. But the women who hold these positions are a vastly different group from those who had been employed previously. Prior to World War II, employment for white, married, middle-class women was virtually unheard of. Today, it has become the norm for many women throughout most of their lives.

World War II did not cause the change in a direct way, but it did create the context in which a different pattern of behavior evolved. It provided a crucial catalyst toward breaking up an old system of economic roles and setting in motion a new one.

Along with much of present-day management theory, the corporate woman—the counterpart of the man in the gray flannel suit—is a post-World War II phenomenon. To be sure, there were always traditional female professionals. Notables in the last half-century were: pediatrician Virginia Apgar, celebrated anthropologist Margaret Mead, sociologist Mary Parker Follett, distinguished jurist Jennie Loitman Barron, and many others. But there were no management women as we know them today. The closest one could come to a management woman prior to World War II was a female entrepreneur like the creative and financially astute

Madame Rubinstein or academic consultant to management Lillian Gilbreth, or the first female cabinet member, Frances Perkins.

People tend to forget that it wasn't until 1963 that the Harvard Business School, traditional training-ground for the country's business leaders, accepted its first female student. Moreover, until the mid 1970s management texts did not even suggest the possibility that women could be managers. Even now there are few case materials available depicting women in realistic leadership roles.

Today, women make up more than 47 percent of the labor force. Yet a scant one percent can be seriously considered top management and five to six percent middle management. Although there have been competent female managers at the lower levels of management for the last 25 years, *not one woman* has made it to the top of a Fortune 500 company by climbing the corporate ladder.

It should surprise no one, therefore, that in 1976 when *Business Week* decided to do a feature story on the 100 top corporate women in the country, they had a devil of a time finding them. Irene Pave, then editor of the corporate women's pages, revealed that close to 100 stringers canvassed the country in search of the elusive corporate woman. Find them she did; and in so doing she provided the author with the unique population for this study of mentoring.

THE NATURE OF MENTORING IN WOMEN

Primarily, our purpose in conducting our study was to find out whether mentoring has been a significant part of the career development of these successful female managers.*

Beyond that, we wanted to learn as much as possible about the nature of the relationship. So we focused upon the following set of research questions:

- Is the mentor/protégé relationship as described by Daniel J. Levinson and Harry Levinson cited in Chapter One different as it applies to female managers?

*The terms "mentor" and "mentoring" are used here in the broadest sense to include all of the dyads in the continuum described by Shapiro, Haseltine and Rowe, referred to in Chapter One. The adjective "successful" is specified in the criteria used to identify the research subjects in the following section.

- Are there stages of socialization or patterns of behavior within the mentor/protégé relationship that can be clearly identified?
- Do mentors and their protégés have shared values, attitudes and goals?
- Are mentors former protégés?
- Is the issue of voluntary association important? The issue of initiation?
- Is sexuality addressed in the mentor/protégé relationship?

The criteria used in the exhaustive national search conducted by *Business Week* were essentially the same as those used in this study. The woman had to be: (1) one of the highest-ranking female managers in the company; (2) a recognized professional in her industry; and (3) one whose annual salary exceeded $30,000.

There were a number of women in the *Business Week* survey group, such as Mary Roebling, Katherine Graham and Mary Wells, who are not corporate women in the sense intended for this research and were, therefore, excluded. While they are well-educated and extraordinarily competent women, they did not climb any corporate ladder. In the case of Mary Roebling and Katherine Graham, both inherited the chief executive officer's (CEO's) position from their husbands. Mary Wells, blocked in her advance to the top, took the entrepreneurial route.

For purposes of this study, widows of CEO's, heiresses and entrepreneurs were exempt. Corporate women were defined as those women whose career development took place within the organizational context and who were therefore subject to the constraints of an organizational hierarchy. Since 1976, the number of corporate women who met the criteria noted may have changed and, therefore, the population of experienced practitioners may be somewhat more or less than 100.

Purposes of the Mail Survey

Primarily, the mail survey of all subjects was intended to serve as a simple screening device to distinguish those who have had a mentor from those who have not. In addition, the biographical data were intended to provide the basis for demographic comparison between the two groups.

For example: Are there educational differences in the level and type of preparation for management, i.e., MBA, JD, or engineering degrees versus liberal arts degrees? Are there strategic advancement differences, i.e., staff versus line progression? Does age appear to be a factor? How?

Daniel J. Levinson says that men map out their career strategies (the dream) in their early twenties and further concludes that men do not have mentors after the age of 40. On the other hand, Hennig says that most businesswomen defer serious commitment to career goals until their mid-thirties. These alternative time frames suggest some interesting outcomes and their possible implications. Clearly, if women start their career strategies later, one possible outcome is that they may never attract mentors, since it has been observed that men will not risk involvement with a protégé unless there is strong evidence that the achievements of the protégé will bring credit to the mentor. Less time on the track may be perceived as a serious handicap for a female protégé. Still another possible outcome is that women may have mentors well into their forties because of the ten-year lag in their commitment decision.

Age differences between mentor and protégé also suggest some interesting comparisons. While for men the mentor is reported ordinarily to be some 5 to 15 years older than the protégé, it might well be that for women that age gap is much smaller or is reversed. Given that one of the attractions in this relationship is presumed to be the status and power of the mentor, it is conceivable that a woman may be the protégé of a man who is her contemporary or is even younger than she.

These are but a few of the dimensions that were explored from the comparisons obtained from the demographics requested in the survey. The remainder of the survey consisted of open-ended questions which were designed to lay the foundation for the subsequent in-depth interviews.

From those women who identified a sponsor or a mentor as a significant developmental figure, ten women were to be chosen for subsequent personal interviews. In addition, recognizing the possibility that some of the women might feel pressure to deny that they had a mentor or might choose to "forget" the relationship, five women from the non-mentor group were also to be selected for interviewing.

While our purpose here was not specifically to compare successful women who have had mentors with successful women who have not had mentors, the interviews with the non-mentor group served as a control and contributed to the richness of our analysis and/or understanding of the mentoring process. For example: If indeed these women had no mentoring, how were their needs for support, direction, reinforcement, identification, etc., met?

From the list of 100 women identified in *Business Week*, 13 women were eliminated because they were known to be entrepreneurs or heiresses.

The survey was mailed to the remaining 87 women. During the several months this investigation was underway, three prominent appointments were announced to the press. The names of these women were added to the list, making the total of top management women surveyed 90.

Survey Responses

On the first pass, 21 completed surveys were returned. After three weeks another mailing and follow-up telephone calls elicited another four responses. The total number of completed and usable survey responses, either by mail, phone, or in person was 35. Note the summary of survey responses in Table 2.1.

TABLE 2.1. Survey Responses

Total Mailing		90
Completed by mail	25	
Completed in person	10	
Total Completed and Usable Surveys		35
Returned marked "unknown"	10	
Returned with "regrets"	3	
Completed but not used (an entrepreneur)	1	
Total Survey Response		49

Ten of the surveys were returned marked "unknown" or "no longer employed." For each of these returns, a letter was sent to the company personnel director asking for a forwarding address. In only one case was this information provided. It was for Esther Peterson, Special Assistant to the President for Consumer Affairs. All other personnel officers responded indicating "no knowledge."

The personnel officer at Citibank, for example, sent back a form letter with Name, Social Security Number, and dates of employment filled in, and with the entries: *Last position*: vice president; *Remarks*: none." Yet the letter was personally signed by the personnel director. At Amtrak the personnel director wrote on the bottom of the survey letter: "Sorry, *absolutely* no information on the above mentioned subject."

The kind of response and the choice of words used say something about the people involved, the companies they were employed by and their interactions. But what?

Is this generally disinterested attitude toward senior managers and former vice presidents typical or atypical of these companies? Is it indicative of the low esteem in which the individual was held or of some unpleasantness which occurred when they severed their relationship? Or was it simply a "bad day" for the person responding to the inquiry? If the inquiry were made regarding a male executive would these companies have felt a stronger obligation to forward a professional inquiry?

These are moot questions, but nonetheless important questions to reflect upon. The attitudes and perceptions of male managers, especially lower level personnel managers, were an obstacle in gaining access to information. While I would speculate that those attitudes may be unconscious, they nevertheless can be very real barriers to the timely and earned advancement of women.

Senior executives who are female, it would appear, are dismissed in their departure as cavalierly as a file clerk or a switchboard operator. In contrast, male executives are pampered in the exit process and thereafter. There is an implicit obligation to "cover" for the male executive moving out, whatever the circumstances surrounding his departure. Movement, even to the competition, is not permanently viewed as a defection, but merely a shifting of alliances. The movement of women, on the other hand, is apparently viewed by low-level personnel people, at least, as either inconsequential, terminal or both.

There is a risk here, not only for women and their advancement, but also for the corporation. Senior executives who have a genuine concern about the development of executive talent in their organization will want to be more sensitive to the many subtle and seemingly innocuous ways in which the reputation of a female manager can be undermined—even after she has left.

Three women wrote letters of acknowledgment saying that while they appreciated the importance of the project, the demands on their time would not permit their participation. One of the completed surveys was not used because it was from an entrepreneur who was not identified as such before the mailing.

Interviews in Depth

The format of the 15 interviews was informal, open-ended and relatively unstructured. The underlying purpose, of course, was to encourage the women to explore their memories and to explain in as great detail as possible the nature, depth and unique qualities of the relationships which they identified as significant in their career development. The interviews were tape-recorded and usually lasted about two hours—some lasted about an hour and forty-five minutes, others lasted almost three hours. Most of the interviews were conducted at corporate headquarters in the woman's office. One was conducted in the St. Francis Hotel in San Francisco. Another was conducted on the Babson College campus in Wellesley because the woman was in town to attend a trustees' meeting. Two interviews with members of the non-mentor group were conducted over the phone.

While flexibility of approach was maintained throughout the interviews, we were guided in our inquiry by our specific purpose: (1) to identify specific activities and/or behaviors, perceptions and feelings recalled by the subjects as their own and those of their mentor; and (2) to note changes in the relationship over time.

The following specific questions—some of which appeared at the end of the survey and for which we had at least a superficial response—served as "lead-ins" for deeper investigation.

- Is there some one person (or perhaps more than one person) who stands out in your mind as the one who *most* influenced your career development at a critical juncture?
- In what ways was this person influential or instrumental in your career progress and development?

The first question served to identify a key figure not labeled a "mentor" or a "sponsor," because often the subject may not have consciously thought about the significant person in her life in those terms. The second question attempted to focus the subject's attention upon the details of a process of influence. What we were looking for here were specific activities (public behaviors) engaged in by the mentor that were perceived by the protégé as beneficial, as well as the behaviors and feelings of the protégé in response.

- How did you happen to meet? On the job? Socially? At school? By chance?
- Did you seek this person out subsequently? Did he seek you out? Were subsequent meetings situational?
- Was this person a member of the same organization? Is he now? Was this person related to you in any way? Is he now?

These questions opened up the issue of initiation into the mentor/protégé relationship. We could then begin to discuss the perceptions, behaviors and feelings recalled from the first meeting and subsequently.

- Is there something that particularly attracted you to this person?
- How would you describe this person?

The key word here is *attraction*. After the survey revealed whether the subject answered these questions in terms of personality traits, professional skills or feelings, she was asked to describe the person in alternative terms. Some of the follow-up questions were:

- How do you think you were perceived by this person initially? Now?
- Were you ever consciously aware that this person was preparing you for "bigger and better" things? How?
- Did you have a specific goal? Did you both share this goal?
- Would you say you and this person were alike? Different? In what ways?
- Is there a difference in your ages? How much? Do you think this influenced the relationship in any way? How?
- How long did the relationship last? Are you still in touch?
- What was the most satisfying or rewarding aspect of this relationship for you? What do you think was the most satisfying or rewarding aspect of this relationship for this person?
- How do you know? Did you ever discuss this with one another?
- What were some of the negative, trying or disappointing aspects of this relationship for you?
- How do you know? Did you ever discuss these issues with one another?
- What advice would you give to young women coming up through the corporate ranks today regarding their involvement in mentor/protégé relationships?

Needless to say, any one of the foregoing questions might have been followed up or not, depending upon the response. Sometimes they were posed differently later on in the interview or dropped altogether if that seemed appropriate. If the issue was critical, as it was in one or two cases, the subject was broached again by telephone sometime later. In one instance, the subject wrote a letter following the interview responding to the question which was never asked explicitly.

In view of the fact that the mentor/protégé relationship can best be described as a "love relationship" (D. Levinson, 1978), which often leaves in its wake ambivalent feelings, the interviewer's skill, credibility and discretion were important facilitators in the establishment of the requisite rapport.

Interview Strategy and Responses

Rather than waiting for all of the surveys to dribble in before separating out the mentor and non-mentor groups, a potential list of interviewees was chosen from leading companies representing a broad cross-section of American industry. They were employed by firms engaged in: advertising, banking, broadcasting, the electrical and electronics field, finance and investments, food, manufacturing, publishing, retailing, services, and utilities. From a geographic perspective, organizations with corporate headquarters located on both the east and west coasts, as well as in the midwest, were chosen.

The 15 women selected for possible interview were contacted directly by phone. It was our assumption that there would be a 50/50 chance that the person called would have a mentor and would be willing to be interviewed. Presumably, then, we could schedule at least ten interviews without depending upon survey returns. More importantly, it was our sense that at the top management level, a proactive approach would be most effective in securing the interviews. Indeed, calling "cold"—without introduction or survey response from the prospective interviewees—proved to be a most advantageous strategy.

The women expressed genuine interest in the research subject, but only a few recalled having received the survey. They indicated, however, that they receive many such inquiries, and generally do not commit the time to respond. There was a certain expression of regret about dismissing these inquiries indiscriminately.

It was at this point that the researcher took the initiative to repeat in a personal way what was stated formally in the cover letter:

> A critical part of the research involves a survey of experienced and prominent practitioners, to be followed by a selected sample of personal interviews. You are one of the 100 top businesswomen in the country. As such, your career history and personal insights can contribute *what no one else can* to our understanding of the career development of women in top management. I appreciate the fact that since there are so few women at the highest levels, this does put a burden on those who have achieved distinction—but a proud one, I think.

Significantly, none of the women contacted personally refused to participate in the study. Only one woman eventually withdrew and that appeared to be a corporate policy decision and not a personal one. At the time, her company was engaged in a precedent-setting class-action suit with the federal government.

The biggest problem encountered in setting up the interviews was scheduling. Each interview required blocking off a two-hour segment of uninterrupted time. Appointments were scheduled, and often cancelled at the last minute and rescheduled. Since most of the interviews required plane travel, resolving the scheduling problem tested the flexibility and good will of both the researcher and the interviewee.

When an interview finally took place, the problem became one of establishing intimate rapport quickly. Since some of these prominent women had been interviewed by journalists many times before, it was conceivable that they might be defensive or that their responses might seemed contrived. How to establish a rapport based on mutual respect and trust? The researcher chose to take time at the outset of each interview to summarize her own business background and her motivation for undertaking this research. During this personal exchange, the researcher attempted to reinforce the impression that she conveyed over the phone: in other words, that she was intimately acquainted with the subtleties of corporate life and that they shared much in common. The perception that the researcher was an "insider" made it possible for the women to reveal much more of themselves and their organizational lives than they might have felt free to do otherwise. It was upon this foundation of mutual respect and trust that the interviews were conducted.

A number of women expressed a sense of personal revelation and pleasure at the conclusion of the interviews. For a few the revelation was more painful than pleasurable. As one woman put it, "I never imagined myself talking to anyone about these feelings."

These reactions are noted here because interviewing is an interactive process, and therefore, the interviewer is as much a factor in the substance and content of the interview as the person being interviewed.

Interview Analysis

In our analysis of the interviews we chose to focus upon behaviors, perceptions and feelings because it was our sense that together these three aspects could provide a reasonably coherent picture of the dynamics of a relationship.

Let's take a look now at this unique population of women and see what can be learned from their personal backgrounds, their career development patterns, and the dimensions of their significant relationships.

chapter three

100 top businesswomen: a unique population

The strongest are those who renounce their own times and become a living part of those yet to come. The strongest and the rarest.

MILOVAN DJILAS

The women who comprise the population of this study—the "100 top businesswomen" in the country—is a small yet elegant group. Some are very prominent and visible women, and as such, have received considerable press attention. Others, though equally prominent in their fields, are relatively unknown. So before we proceed to analyze the experiences of our interview sample, it might be enlightening to know something about the background characteristics of the population from which our sample is drawn. What can be said about these top management women as a group in terms of their educational preparation for management, their organizational experience, their titles, salaries, ages and so on? How do they compare with their male counterparts?

Moving on to the specific topic of this study: Do these women have mentors? And if so, what are some of the general characteristics of these relationships? How do these characteristics compare with the data available regarding the mentoring relationships of top management men?

This chapter, then, will report the results of the general survey with regard to these questions in both tabular and descriptive form in the first section. The general hypothesis and associated questions will be addressed in the second section. And a summary of the findings, together with a comparison of this survey with comparable surveys, will be provided in the last section. For purposes of simplicity and clarity, the terms "mentor" and "non-mentor" groups will be used to distinguish those who say they have had a significant supportive relationship in their business careers from those who say they have not. First, a look at the unique population from which our sample is drawn.

DEMOGRAPHIC CHARACTERISTICS OF THE SURVEY GROUP

The general profile of the participants in this survey is in effect the composite profile of top businesswomen in the country, presented in Table 3.1.

Education

As a group, the women are college-educated, though by no means is a degree an entrance requirement for this group. Four women (11.4%) reported no college degree.

As undergraduates, by far the largest percentage (72.4%) chose liberal arts majors, which is consistent with the national averages for all college women. However, the remaining 27.6 percent chose majors such as economics (2), business administration (3), physics (3), chemistry (1), mathematics (1), and meteorology (1).

Fifty-seven percent (57.1%) have graduate degrees. Twenty-five percent (25.8%) have an MS or an MA degree; seventeen percent (17.1%) hold an MBA degree; eight percent (8.6%) an LLB or JD degree; and five percent (5.7%) a Ph.D.

More than half of the women (55.9%) participated in continuing education programs which were job-related. Some were company-sponsored management development programs, others were university or institute courses designed to develop a specific skill.

Marital Status

Contrary to the pejorative stereotype of the "old maid" executive, 45.7 percent of the survey group are currently married, and that percentage jumps to 57.1 percent if you include those who have been divorced. Of those who are now or who have been married, 65 percent have children.

Organizational Experience

In general these women have spent the better part of their working lives in one company. The average number of years with their present employer is 15 years. There is a very broad range, however, from a low of one year to a high of 35 years.

Their average age is 47.8; and the average salary (71.4%) is over $50,000.

TABLE 3.1. Profile of Top Businesswomen

	Frequency	Frequency (percent)
Personal		
Education		
No College	4	11.4
BA or BS	11	31.4
MA or MS	9	25.8
MBA	6	17.1
LLB or JD	3	8.6
Ph.D.	2	5.7
Marital Status		
Never Married	15	42.9
Married	16	45.7

TABLE 3.1. (continued)

	Frequency	Frequency (percent)
Personal		
Divorced	4	11.4
Average Age		47.8 years
Organizational		
Title		
President	3	8.6
Vice President	26	74.3
Other	6	17.1
Salary		
$31,000-40,000	6	17.1
$41,000-50,000	4	11.4
Over $50,000	25	71.4

Average Number of Years with Same Employer: 15 years

How did they make their way through the organizational ranks? The majority of women came up through *staff* positions. Though many of them are now vice presidents, they are vice presidents in a staff function, which is the top of that functional hierarchy. Most do not have the diversity of experience to transfer to the line.* Note Table 3.2.

Nine of the respondents reported having a "mixed" career path; that is, they have held positions at various times which were, strictly speaking, line functions. However, a review of these cases indicates that these digressions to the line were brief. The brevity of the experience is not as impor-

---

*Generally, line positions are those functions essential to the conduct of the business. In a manufacturing firm, for example, the foreman, plant manager, division manager, operations vice president and president might comprise the chain of command. Authority and power are inherent in the job function. Staff positions, on the other hand, are ancillary or support functions, such as, accounting, personnel, research and development and the like. Staff positions are essentially advisory in nature and have no power in and of themselves.

For a more detailed treatment of Line and Staff functions see Litterer, Joseph A., *An Introduction to Management*, John Wiley & Sons, Inc. New York 1978.

TABLE 3.2. Career Progression

	Frequency	Frequency (percent)
Staff	22	62.9
Line	2	5.7
Mixed	9	25.7
Other	2	5.7
Total	35	100.0

tant as the experience itself. For some, it was an early introductory working experience that—for whatever reason—was not followed through. For others, it was a significant departure. It gave them the breadth of experience needed at an appropriate time in their careers so that later they could be seriously considered top management candidates. The two cases labeled "other" had no prior corporate experience before becoming corporate vice presidents. They had previously made their marks in the legal and non-profit sector.

IS AFFIRMATIVE ACTION A POSITIVE FORCE?

The respondents appear to be split on the importance of affirmative action legislation on their career progress, as Table 3.3 indicates.

TABLE 3.3. Impact of Affirmative Action

	Frequency	Frequency (percent)
None	12	34.3
Minimal	7	20.0
Some	11	31.4
Substantial	4	11.4
Greatest	1	2.9
Total:	35	100.0

The group (54.3%) who say that affirmative action had little or no impact on their career progress is comprised of an interesting mixture. There are those who are over 50 years old. These women say the impact was "minimal" or "none" because their careers were "well underway before affirmative action was even thought of," as one woman explains. This seems justified.

On the other hand, there are those few women who are in their thirties who claim it had little or no impact. This seems curious in view of the fact that their entire working experience has occurred during the post-civil rights period from 1964 to the present. It may just be that they may not have been aware of significant changes in the business environment because they had no other time frame with which to compare the period of their working experience.

Last but not least, several of these women who say affirmative action had little or no significance in their career progress are those who also reported having had no supportive professional relationships. (This is discussed in detail in Chapter Eight.)

While the survey respondents in general and the interviewees in particular were clear in acknowledging their own expertise and their ability to handle the positions they now hold, they felt that the tangible rewards, such as title and commensurate salary, would not have been forthcoming had it not been for affirmative action. Forty-five percent (45.7%) indicated that affirmative action had at least some impact on their career progress.

The interviewees, in defense of their company's management, hasten to add that this lack of recognition and promotion was not through any overt or conscious withholding of rewards on the part of their superiors, but was simply "the way it was" at the time. Let us now look at the prevalence of mentoring relationships in this group.

DO TOP BUSINESSWOMEN HAVE MENTORS?

Now that we have a sense of what the general profile of the top management woman is and what her views are concerning affirmative action, what can be said about the prevalence of mentoring?

Better than 85 percent (85.7%) of the respondents reported having had a relationship which most influenced their career development. Therefore, the general hypothesis—that mentoring has been a significant part of the development of successful female managers—is confirmed. Significantly, 82.9 percent of these women are at least vice presidents. Three are presidents of substantial subsidiaries of major companies. Note Table 3.4.

TABLE 3.4. Prevalence of Supportive Relationships

	Frequency	Frequency (percent)
Mentor	30	85.7
Non-mentor	5	14.3
Total:	35	100.0

The survey respondents appear to have had between two and three (2.6) supportive relationships that could be described as mentoring and/or sponsoring in nature. The relationships were, on average, of 11 to 12 years' duration. The shortest was of two years' duration; the longest relationship reported was 49 years. It is worth noting that reported relationships of longer than 15 years were either familial in nature or relationships which, though still ongoing, have passed beyond the mentoring phase. Adjusting for these disparities in the data, the average number of years' duration appears to be about ten.

Over 83 percent (83.3%) of these supportive relationships were with men. The foregoing data is summarized in Table 3.5.

TABLE 3.5. Characteristics of Supportive Relationships

Average number	2.6
Average duration	10 years
Gender of mentor or sponsor	83.3% male

Where Is a Mentor to be Found?

For the most part (80%) the participants in these supportive relationships met on the job. The remaining 20 percent met socially, at school, or by chance. Note frequencies in Table 3.6.

TABLE 3.6. Initiating Encounters

	Frequency	Frequency (percent)
On the job	24	80.0
Socially	1	3.3
At school	1	3.3
By chance	1	3.3
Other	3	10.0
Total:	32	100.0

Of the three cases labeled "other," two of the mentoring relationships were with a parent—one a mother, one a father. In the third case, the protégé was for many years the owner of a service business where her mentor, a woman, was a client.

Do Former Protégés Become Mentors?

In answer to the question "Have you ever been a mentor?" 80 percent answered "yes." The surveyed women appear to be supportive of promising men and women alike. There seems to be no gender preference. Sixty-four percent (64.3%) reported having mentored both men and women; 21 percent (21.3%) reported mentoring women only; and 14 percent (14.3%) men only.

COMPARISON WITH SURVEY OF MALE EXECUTIVES

How do these findings compare with the findings of Heidrick & Struggles, who surveyed the nation's leading business executives? There are some striking parallels and some equally striking differences.

Of the 1250 executives in the Heindrick & Struggles sample, less than one percent, or something less than 12, were women. The exact number was unspecified. (Significantly, all of these women reported having mentors.) So for all intents and purposes we shall view this study as a survey of male executives.

Heidrick & Struggles found that mentor/protégé relationships are fairly extensive among the male elite of the business world. Sixty-three percent (63.5%) reported having had a significant professional relationship whereas 85 percent of our sample of top management women reported significant professional relationships. It may be that mentoring relationships are more prevalent among women who choose to scale the corporate heights than they are among men with similar aspirations.

There are a number of interesting parallels, however, with respect to: how many mentoring relationships a single career can accommodate; how long such a relationship usually lasts; where mentors and protéges are most likely to encounter one another; and how old a "successful" executive is likely to be.

Both men and women average between two and three mentors in their lives and for the most part, the mentors are men. The relationships generally last at least ten years. Though a mentor may be thought of as an organizational "teacher," there appear to be surprisingly few teachers reported as mentors in either study. The place to meet a mentor is definitely "on the job." Moreover, to become a successful executive, either male or female, it takes a good many years on the job before one reaches the top. The average age of both men and women who have reached the top management ranks is between 47 and 49.

Now let us consider some interesting differences. On average, the female executives are better educated yet lower paid than male executives. Almost 60 percent of the women in this study have advanced degrees; almost 50 percent of the men hold advanced degrees. While 71 percent of the female executives earn over $50,000 annually, 96 percent of the male executives earn over $50,000 dollars annually.

With a little healthy cynicism one might conclude that women are always paid less—even women executives. However, one ought not to overlook the fact that this substantial gap in salary may also be a reflection of staff salaries versus line salaries. Traditionally, salaries in dollars are higher for line officers than for staff officers; so too are the perquisites.

One of the interesting findings of the Heidrick & Struggles survey is that most male protégés still have a good relationship with their mentors. "Nearly 6 in 10 describe their current relationship as 'friendly'," say

Heidrick & Struggles, "and more than 3 in 10 describe it as 'close'." This outcome is consistent with our findings for the women whom we interviewed who had mentors.

Given that men are generally more reluctant than women to express their feelings, one might speculate that the actual number of "friendly" and/or "close" relationships is even higher than reported. These findings seem to differ with Daniel Levinson's observation that "an intense mentor relationship ends with conflict and bad feelings on both sides." More on this point in the coming chapters.

COMPARISON WITH PHILLIPS' SURVEY OF WOMEN EXECUTIVES

It is difficult to make detailed or extensive comparisons with the Phillips' survey data of women managers and executives given that the samples are so different. Forty-seven percent of the women in the Phillips survey group do not meet the salary criterion used in this study: i.e., the woman must earn an annual salary of at least $30,000. Twenty-four percent of the Phillips' survey group are in the "owner, partner, chairperson, board director, president" category, and therefore do not meet a second criterion of our study: i.e., entrepreneurs and heiresses are excluded. And last but not least, the Phillips' study includes both full- and part-time corporate employees. Our study involves *only* full-time, practicing managers.

It is not surprising, therefore, that the background data of the women in the two studies is very different. The average age of the women in the Phillips' sample is 57, as opposed to 47 in our study. The average level of education in the Phillips study is two years of college as opposed to an advanced degree in our study. And the majority of women in the Phillips' study earn less than $30,000 annually as opposed to over $50,000 annually in our sample.

The only similarity, in very general terms, is that 61.5 percent of the Phillips' survey respondents reported they had experienced a mentoring relationship, as opposed to 85 percent in our sample.

The implications here are unclear, but one might hazard a guess. It might be inferred that the population of our study, practicing female managers in top management, is a subset of the population used in the Phillips' study. And if one were inclined to take a leap of faith, one might conclude that the higher up the corporate hierarchy one goes, the greater the likelihood that one has, or has had, a mentor.

SUMMARY OF FINDINGS AND POSSIBLE IMPLICATIONS

In general, then, it can be said that women who reach the top management ranks have had a mentoring relationship of one kind or another. Moreover, they are following in their mentors' footsteps by becoming mentors themselves.

The fact that the vast majority of these relationships occur on the job suggests that the initiating situation is task-related. The proximity and frequency of interaction supports the growth of positive sentiments between the participants.

For the most part, the mentor is a man, which suggests that one of the attractions may be the power of the senior member. Senior here refers to status in the organizational hierarchy, not chronological age. This "power" is all-inclusive, consisting of personal power in terms of charisma, expertise and status, as well as access to resources such as time, money, and information. In view of the fact that women in positions of power are so few, this outcome was predictable.

The fact that 13 percent of the mentors or sponsors reported by the survey group were women was not predictable. This outcome suggests some interesting opportunities for future research. It may be that women in positions of power are more inclined than men to offer support to another woman, a conclusion which flies in the face of the Queen Bee theory. On the other hand, women may have a different set of values against which to measure power than men do. Or perhaps the pivotal factor may simply be situational.

One of the most significant findings, however, is that the channel for advancement for men and women is different. Men who reach top management make their career climb up the *line*—where power is inherent in the chain of command and is clearly defined. In contrast, women who reach the top management ranks make their career advances through the *staff*—where power by definition is advisory, and therefore is a function of personal influence—a very tenuous kind of power at best.

This outcome suggests a number of interesting implications. It may be that the staff is the more easily accessible channel of advancement. Because these staff positions are regarded as secondary power positions in organizations, it may be that they are perceived as more "suitable" for women. Therefore, fewer barriers, real and psychological, exist. On the other hand, this outcome could simply suggest that educationally, the majority of these women were better prepared for staff positions (72.4% were liberal arts majors) than they were for line positions (27.6% were math, science or business majors).

In order to gain insight into what constitutes a mentoring relationship in top management, Chapter Four will analyze the results of in-depth interviews with ten of the distinguished women in this survey group who reported having had a significant professional relationship. The process of mentoring in which they were engaged will be described in detail.

chapter four

The protégés

It takes 20 years to make an overnight success.
EDDIE CANTOR

A PROFILE OF THE STUDY GROUP

The women interviewed were chosen from an industrial and geographic cross-section of American business. They are among the 100 top businesswomen in the country, and they are managers in some of the nation's leading corporations: American Telephone & Telegraph Co., Chase Manhattan Bank, Gaf Corp., General Electric, Jewel Companies, John Hancock Insurance Co., Lockheed, Ogilvy-Mather, Inc., Pacific Gas & Electric, RCA Corp., Time, Inc., and others.

All of the women interviewed have reached at least the vice-presidential level, as shown in Table 4.1. Three have become the president or chief executive officer of a significant subsidiary of the parent company. All ten women, with one exception, reached the vice-presidential level through a series of staff positions. One or two waffled a little, but the overall pattern is clearly staff.

TABLE 4.1. General Profile: Ten Successful Female Managers with Mentors

Title	At least Vice President	100%
Career progression	Staff	90%
Education	Graduate degree	60%
Average number of years with company	22	
Salary	Over $50,000	80%
Age	50's	50%
Marital status	Married	50%

Of course, in companies as large as some of those in which these women made their careers, even the vice president of a staff function becomes a line manager in effect.

There is only one woman of the ten who progressed through the line. Moreover, she is the only one who was a business/marketing major as an undergraduate, and is one of the three who are now chief executive officers.

All are college graduates, and six of them have attended graduate school. Significantly, all of the graduate degrees are in work-related fields. With one exception, those who went on to graduate school were the ones who pursued nonstereotypic undergraduate majors, such as chemistry, physics, meteorology, economics, and mathematics. The one exception has a political science undergraduate degree, but her master's degree is also in a work-related field.

Despite this apparent educational and organizational fit, nine of the ten women started their careers as low-level functionaries: secretaries, clerks, and the like. Only one, the youngest, started as a management trainee fresh out of graduate school with an MBA. The specific entry-level positions are noted in Table 4.2, coupled with the level of educational preparation brought to the respective positions.

It is important to point out that the positions listed above are not necessarily the first job ever held, rather they are the first job held in the firm in which the interviewees worked for the major portion of their careers to date.

As a group they remained with their respective organizations an average of 22 years—a low of 9 and a high of 36 years.

Six of the women—including those with and those without graduate degrees—participated in company-sponsored management development

TABLE 4.2. Entry-Level Positions

Position	Educational Preparation
Budget Clerk, Advertising Dept.	English BA, MBA 4 years later
Management Trainee, Credit Dept.	MBA, Finance
Accounting Clerk	BS, Business Administration
Assistant to Staff Meteorologist	BA in Meteorology, MS in process
Engineering Assistant	AB and MS in Physics
Statistical Clerk	BS, Education
Technical Librarian	BS and MS in Chemistry
Copywriter	BA, English
Secretary	AB, English
Public Relations Assistant	BA in Political Science, MA in English

programs at various times in their respective careers. Some of the programs named were: Menninger, Reddin, Levinson et al., as well as some specific skills programs and institutes.

Eight of the women now earn a salary in excess of $50,000. The lowest-paid earns between $31,000 and $40,000. She is also the youngest in age and time in the organization. The highest-paid earns well over $200,000.

Half of the women are in their fifties today; two are in their thirties, two in their forties and one in her sixties. Of the ten women, eight were in their early twenties when they joined their respective companies. Five out of the ten women are married; three of the five have children. (The foregoing details were not incorporated into Table 4.2 because we wanted to preserve the anonymity of the interviewees.)

With respect to supportive relationships they experienced, the data in Table 4.3 are revealing.

The women reported having had between two and three relationships which they regarded as significant in their career development. The most anyone reported was four; the least, one. In view of the fact that most of these women spent an average of 22 years in the same company, the number of such supportive relationships experienced seems relatively few (consistent with D. Levinson's finding).

In the case of the most significant relationship among these, the

TABLE 4.3. Supportive Relationships

		Male	Female
General			
Total	26	23	3
Average	2-3		
Most Significant			
Total	10	9	1
Average number of years	10-12		
Average age of mentor	15-18 yrs. senior		

one around which the interview analysis revolves, nine out of ten was with a man; one was with a woman. The relationships generally lasted from 10 to 12 years. This is not to suggest that the relationships are no longer viable. On the contrary, they are ongoing in every case. Only the content of the dialogue has changed. (More on this point in the next chapter.)

On average, the mentor is 15 to 18 years older than the protégé. However, in one case the protégé is older by some six years, and in another case—where the mentor is a woman—they are contemporaries.

In summary, then, there are a number of observations which might be made about the foregoing similarities. First of all, these are exceptional women; most of them had already differentiated themselves from the general population of women when they first entered college. They selected non-stereotypic or typically male majors as undergraduates. Secondly, by going on to graduate school in a work-related field, these women made an investment in their professional development and were well-prepared for their professional careers. Thirdly, they not only maintained a demanding career, but half were married and some had children as well.

Last but not least, the profile of these successful female managers bears a striking resemblance to the profile of their counterparts—successful male managers. A comparison of their profile with that of the chief executive officers of the Fortune 500 companies is revealing. Note Table 4.4.

There are two significant differences between successful male managers and successful female managers:

1. Traditionally, men make their way to the top of the management hierarchy through the line. Indeed, 80 percent of the men in the Fortune group came up through the financing, marketing, engineering, and production ranks. In contrast, 90 percent of these women progressed through the staff ranks, often as "assistant to" or trailing close behind their mentors.

TABLE 4.4. Comparison of Successful Male Managers and Successful Female Managers

	Males	Females
College	95%	100%
Graduate degree	58%	60%
Career progression: line	80%	10%
Career progression: staff	20%	90%
Average number of years with company	25	22
Salaries in excess of $50,000	96%	80%
Age	50	50

Source: The male statistics were extrapolated from Charles G. Burch, "A Group Profile of the Fortune 500 Chief Executive," *Fortune*, Vol. 92, No. 5, May 1976.

Only at the very top were two of them able to shift to the line by stepping into the shoes of their boss.

2. Most men with such credentials, i.e., graduate degrees in work-related fields, are placed on the "fast track" from day one. They rarely start out as clerks, secretaries or librarians, and seldom serve such long tenure at the lower levels of the organization.

While there also appears to be a disparity in the salaries noted in Table 4.4, it is our sense that at this juncture in their respective careers it is not a male/female difference, but rather a reflection of the traditionally lower salaries paid to staff officers as opposed to line officers. Some of the possible reasons for these differences were discussed in Chapter Three and will become apparent as the organizational and societal context in which these relationships developed are described by the protégés themselves.

As a group, then, the protégés are well-educated, achievement-oriented women who came into their respective organizations with a strong concept of self, though not necessarily with any great expectations.

PHASES IN MENTOR/PROTÉGÉ RELATIONSHIPS

The pattern of interactions in which the protégés and mentors engaged proceeds through a series of three phases which have been labeled Initiation, Development, and Termination.

Essentially, the Initiation Phase deals with the questions: Who found whom? How? Was there some attraction? If so, what was it? In other words, what precipitated the relationship and what were the subsequent interactions about: i.e., what is happening when we look at the behaviors of the mentor, the protégés' perceptions of those behaviors, and the feelings engendered by their interaction?

Once established, the relationship progresses into a Development Phase. During this stage, all of the growth-facilitating behaviors and the concomitant perceptions and feelings of the previous stage are reinforced and some new ones are introduced. The bulk of the interactions takes place during this stage. This is a period of tremendous professional growth for the protégé, and for the mentor too. It is a period of ambivalent feelings fraught with emotional complexity.

The Termination Phase is in reality a period of transition. The relationship as it was developed and maintained over a period of time begins to change. The functional aspects of the relationship give way to what are largely personal exchanges. The participants move from a mentor/protégé relationship toward a compeer relationship. Such a change must take place if the relationship is to continue to grow.

While these general phases in the mentoring process can be differentiated, the boundaries of each are flexible, and clearly, there are transitional phases. (As noted in Chapter One, the Phillips' study identifies six phases.)

These phases, Initiation, Development, and Termination, are not so precise that in a particular instance a specific behavior may not occur in the next or the preceding phase. The behaviors, perceptions and feelings of one phase sometimes overlap another phase, and the difference may only be a matter of degree.

Our sense is that there is no specific timetable to this progression. The time spent in one phase or another is influenced by a host of personal and situational variables. While for this sample of women the process of mentoring as a dynamic function from Initiation through Termination lasted on average between 10 to 12 years, it is entirely possible for the process to run its course in a much shorter period of time—or for that matter, a much longer period of time.

Each of these phases—Initiation, Development, and Termination—will be described in detail in the following chapters, showing exactly what behaviors, perceptions and feelings are dominant during each particular phase and how they relate to one another.

chapter five

The pygmalion syndrome: initiation

> There is something that is much more scarce, something rarer than ability. It is the ability to recognize ability.
> ROBERT HALF

THE MENTORS

Before describing and discussing the behaviors that mentors engaged in, it might be enlightening to have a sense of what kind of people they were—or more to the point, how they were perceived by their protégés in the organizational context.

As noted earlier, the women in this study are extraordinary in their own right. But their mentors were perceived to be larger-than-life. They were seen as brilliant, charismatic, physically attractive, boundlessly energetic, innovative, totally inspiring human beings. They expected only as much as they themselves were willing and capable of giving, and this posed a problem for some because their abilities were formidable. They appeared to be so far ahead of everyone around them that the people who had the good fortune to work for them considered it a distinct privilege. As one women puts it: "He is a phenomenon." It is through this perceptual prism that the protégés viewed their mentors' behavior.

INITIATION: PHASE I

Repeated Themes In the Behavior of Mentors

Each of the ten mentor/protégé relationships identified was initiated by the mentor and for the most part was developed within a single organization. (However, some of these organizations were of a size to be considered worlds in themselves.) Most of the mentors (nine out of ten) became at some point the direct supervisors of their protégés, but not initially. The protégés came into their respective organizations in a variety of ways, for the most part unobtrusively and inconspicuously.

So what was it that precipitated this relationship?

	Frequency
● Recognized protégé's ability/talent	(10)
● Sets especially high standards of performance	(10)
● Extremely demanding	(10)
● Encouraging (seldom verbally)	(9)

FIGURE 1. Repeated Themes in the Behavior of Mentors: Initiation, Phase I.

As noted in Figure 1, the relationship was precipitated by an awareness on the part of the mentor that here, in the protégé, was a person of ability, someone who performed above average and had potential. While the nature of this potential may have been obscure at this point, the behaviors of the mentors suggest that they perceived someone worth bothering about, someone whose ability was worth cultivating. There was no apparent altruism involved. The mentor simply recognized the protégé's ability or talent and acted accordingly.

According to the women themselves:*

> He just happened to see my work and took the trouble to find out who had done it and where I could be located. While I wasn't direct-

---

*Excerpts quoted throughout the chapter were selected on the basis of clarity of thought and succinctness of expression. As a consequence, while all of the women are quoted, some are quoted more often than others.

ly hired by him, he (the founder and CEO) was the one who spotted my talent and saw to it that I was recruited for his company. It was a tremendous step up for someone as young and inexperienced as I was at the time. It was the turning point of my life.

Without a doubt the fact that he (then a department head, later president) appreciated what I could do and liked me was crucial to my development. . . . Verbalization is one of my skills and none of the Ph.D. chemists was capable of writing a report that could be understood by the nontechnical management we had then. I could. You have to understand—incredible as it seems today—at that time technically trained women were only used as librarians.

He was quick to perceive that I worked without too much direction, and I followed through. Even when I didn't know what I was doing, I learned how to do it without supervision to any great extent.

At the time these "recognitions" took place, the proteges were generally many levels of management below the mentor and did not work directly for him. The mentor may or may not yet have become the CEO, but he was already a recognized organizational "star." The following specific description of one of the mentors fits most of them as a group. One need only substitute the appropriate alma mater.

> He was extremely intelligent, a brilliant person with a wide variety of interests. He was articulate, persuasive and had just the right combination of background: Yale undergrad and Harvard MBA. It was clear from the moment he came through the door that he was going to be a sometime president of the company.

Time and time again the protégés stressed the tremendous demands of time, energy and intellect to which they were subjected in their association with the mentor and those who worked with him. In addition, standards of performance were set which tested and stretched the protégés in ways which were totally unanticipated and for which they were often unprepared.

> He just poured it on: budgeting, copy writing, meeting with other people in his place, dealing with salespeople, dealing with service people to save his time. And trusting me. Knowing that I could do it without causing any trouble. . . . He assumed a lot: that I could deliver; and he saw to it that I did.
>
> He expected a lot, not just of me, but of everybody who worked for him. . . . A very, very demanding man.

He was not a man who relished sloppy thinking, poor work, excuses instead of results or any of the other things, so it made for very firm working conditions; but I learned a lot. I was held to standards which were the highest that I've ever had in my life. My academic life, my first job certainly didn't put a strain on me that I couldn't cope with. This was the first time I had to work for someone who really made me sweat.

He was tremendously encouraging because his standards were always so high and there was no persiflage or covering up of his true reaction to anything you did. He did not mince words. You wouldn't expect this kind of standard to be held up for a young and inexperienced person.

The protégés were seldom verbally or explicitly encouraged. In fact, the better they performed, the more they got to do. So why did they continue to work so hard? What was there about the mentors' behaviors at this stage that could be construed as motivating? Why didn't they see their mentors as slave drivers or insatiable workaholics rather than supermen?

Repeated Themes in the Protégés Perception of Mentors' Behavior

As explained earlier, behaviors in and of themselves tell us very little. They merely describe a happening. They offer only a clue as to the meaning of what is happening in terms of the dynamics of a relationship. It is the protégés' perception of those behaviors that gives the behaviors their special meaning.

A look at some of the dominant themes in the protégés' perceptions of the mentors' behaviors will serve to underscore the point: It is not just the behaviors of the mentor that are crucial in developing the relationship; rather it is the meaning attributed to those behaviors by the protégé that is the key to their interaction. (See Figure 2.)

Frequency

- A sense of being molded or created by the mentors (Pygmalion syndrome). (5)
- The pursuit of excellence as a shared value and an intrinsic reward. (9)
- An atmosphere of expectation in which demands are seen as opportunities. (8)

- Self-concept confirmed by association with the mentor. (9)

FIGURE 2. Protégés' Perception of Mentors' Behavior: Initiation, Phase 1.

Each protégé's perception of her mentor's behavior is a very personal one, yet there is great unanimity on one point: their mentors created the opportunity for them to operate outside of the societal norms of the time. They were allowed to participate fully in the "wonderful world of man's work," with all of the dignity that the phrase implies. The symbolism of creation is powerful, but the reality is more powerful still. These were well-educated, intelligent, achievement-oriented women who already possessed a strong sense of self, but who had no real expectations of fulfillment in the sense of actualizing their potential. Is it any wonder, then, that the person who offered the opportunity of fulfillment was perceived as a superman, a miracle worker? Is it any wonder that their achievements under his tutelage came to them as something of a surprise?

While each protégé describes her mentor's behavior from her own unique perspective, their answers suggest something of a Pygmalion syndrome:

> He had sort of a proprietary interest in the precocious little girl he'd discovered. After all, he had invented me. It was very much in his self-interest to prove himself right.

> He was one, two, three, four layers above me. He just simply reached down (gesture) and said, 'All right. You start this and see what you can do with it.' He really brought me into management. It is true. I would never have had the opportunity, if it had not been for him.

> It was his opportunity to take me out of the secretarial mold and put me into another category. If it's not a mold, it's a category. In fact, I was quite surprised to discover my affinity, my seemingly innate ability for marketing. I responded so well to his teaching that it (the latent ability) came as a complete surprise to me.

A stimulating atmosphere of expectation prevailed which opened up options and possibilities for personal fulfillment which were far beyond the limited expectations of these women. The opportunity provided by the mentor was to be given meaningful work to do.

Because the mentor was so demanding and exacting in his standards, simply being able to meet his expectations had intrinsic value for these achievement-oriented women. Thus the work itself became its own reward. Each time the proteges were given more to do, they were encouraged (reinforced) because their sense of self was being confirmed: "Yes, indeed, I am a person of intellect, initiative and responsibility, because he believes I am. And he proves it by trusting me to do work that will live up to his standards and his expectations." Did they resent this apparent overload, this tremendous pressure to perform?

"I sure as hell didn't resent it," says one of the protégés. Some others explain why:

> It (demands and standards) was a rewarding experience, terribly rewarding, because I was using myself in ways I would never have dreamed of. I was being asked to do and bring standards of excellence which certainly nothing in my training had made me ready for. So it was a very satisfactory experience to be doing so many things so meaningfully and so successfully.

> It was always, "Well, all right. Now we need a performance appraisal system and we need it Monday." He just always expected that it would be done. So, you know, you live up to expectations.

> He treated me no differently from any of them (management men). You have to know how unusual that was. It was miraculous. There wasn't another man in the place at that time who would have had the self-confidence.

It seems clear from the foregoing that the protégés concluded that outstanding performance in difficult and challenging situations leads to opportunities to be given more difficult and still more challenging work to do. This pattern of expectation and reward was established early and maintained throughout their careers. Moreover, the work itself was not only of intrinsic value, but it was a symbol of status, power, and respect as well. It was an affirmation.

Repeated Themes in the Feelings Expressed by the Protégés

The full impact of the protégés' perceptions of the mentors' behaviors can more accurately be assessed when the emotional components of these interactions are examined. What were the feelings experienced by these women in the initiation stage of this relationship?

	Frequency
• Gratitude, admiration and respect	(10)
• Excitation by the association with power and its implications	(8)
• A feeling of being somehow "special," worthy of attention, valued	(8)

FIGURE 3. Repeated Themes in the Feelings of Protégés: Initiation, Phase 1.

As noted in Figure 3 above, feelings of gratitude, admiration and respect for the mentor have been clearly enunciated by the protégés and documented in many of the foregoing excerpts, and do not need to be repeated. Let us say simply that feelings of gratitude, admiration and respect are ongoing and persist through every stage of the relationship—feelings which deepen as the relationship progresses. (More on this point in the following chapter.)

The predominant feeling expressed by the women during this initial phase, however, was a tremendous sense of being somehow "special," worthy of attention and valued. To test the reality of that feeling all they needed to do was to look around them. There wasn't another comparable woman in sight. While these women were not distinguished by their salaries, for the most part, they were distinguished by the work they were given to do, and the respect it brought them.

The following excerpts should serve to underscore their feelings of distinction:

> I felt that he saw something more in me than in some of the other people, and that maybe we understood each other a little bit better.
>
> There was this feeling of having to live up to being terrific.
>
> At a very early age I was the only woman in the department. As a matter of fact, for the first 10 to 15 years of my life here, I was the only woman at an executive meeting... I was the only woman doing work not regarded as woman's work.

In evaluating the importance and force of these feelings, one has to appreciate just how unusual it was to have a woman in the management ranks 25 years ago when most of these women were in the Initiation Phase. (Notable exceptions, of course, are those women who were entrepreneurs or whose husbands or fathers owned the business. As noted in Chapter Two, such women were excluded from this study.)

Even the youngest of those interviewed—one whose career in the organization started when she was hired as a trainee in 1970—couldn't help but feel "special." She was the first of the female MBA's brought into the organization flagged for the "fast track"—up to that time reserved exclusively for men. (The implications of the precipitating societal changes will be discussed in a later chapter.)

Heightening this sense of being "special" was the special status these women acquired by their association with the powerful. Indeed, if their mentors were regarded as organizational stars, it was not unreasonable for the protégé to conclude that this association gave her "satellite status." Most of the protégés described the experience as "heady."

> For someone who at that time was on the second level of management, it was sort of a heady experience to have the president saying, "Draw up a chair, sit down, and let's talk about what's happening."
>
> That (accompanying the mentor to important client meetings) was a heady experience for a young girl.
>
> It was just very exciting. Once you've been at the site of power (corporate headquarters) . . . it's heady stuff.

We can only guess at the effect this close association with the powerful had on others with whom these women came in contact in the conduct of their work and in general. In the organizational context, at least, it seems reasonable to conclude that they enjoyed all of the benefits of a "halo effect" as well as some of the detriments of such exclusivity. That is to say, the proteges stood in the reflected glow of their mentors. They were perceived to be women outside the norm. They were regarded as intelligent, competent, innovative—people who possessed many of the positive attributes of the superior person, the mentor. Moreover, the behavior of the mentor towards them was a clear signal to others that they were to be treated differently from the general population of women. They were "special."

The concomitant to this special treatment, of course, was the inevitable isolation that these women experienced in the social structure of the organization (described in greater detail in our discussion of Phase II).

The foregoing behaviors, perceptions and feelings evoked during the Initiation Phase can be viewed as essentially growth-facilitating interactions—ones in which the participants in the interactions, mentor and protégé, are gaining more accurate knowledge about one another and more skill in dealing with one another.

The key element in these growth-facilitating interactions, however, is that challenge is paired with ability. The protégés are stretched by their mentors, but not beyond their ability to perform successfully at this stage. The importance of this balance should not be underestimated. Challenge that is just beyond one's grasp but within one's reach is essential, as early success is a fundamental building block of motivation and the expectation for future success.

Too much responsibility too soon can frustrate and discourage a budding protégé. Too little responsibility can have precisely the same dysfunctional effect, leaving one's competence in question and one's self-esteem bruised.

Let us review for a moment some of the descriptions of the mentors' behaviors in the Initiation Phase as well as the protégés' responses to those behaviors:

> He *assumed* a lot . . . that I could deliver.
> He *expected* a lot.
> He was tremendously *encouraging* (because of his high standards).
> He didn't *mince words*.
> There was this feeling of *having to live up to being terrific*.

The assumption of competence, the encouragement, the feedback, the sense of being "terrific" all underscore the influence of one person's expectations on another's behavior—in this case the mentor's expectations on the protégé's behavior.

Expectations and Performance

Much of the complex interaction which took place between mentor and protégé is explainable by existing behavioral theory.

In examining the career progress of 49 college graduates who were managerial employees of AT&T over a period of five years, Berlew and Hall (1966) discovered that the new manager's relative success, as measured by salary increases and the company's estimate of each man's performance and potential, depended largely on the company's expectations of them.

Berlew and Hall summarized the process as follows:

> Something important is happening in the first year.... Meeting high company expectations in the critical first year leads to the internalization of positive job attitudes and high standards; these attitudes and standards, in turn, would first lead to and be reinforced by strong performance and success in later years. It should also follow that a new manager who meets the challenge of one highly demanding job will be given subsequently a more demanding job and his level of contribution will rise as he responds to the company's growing expectations of him. The key ... is the concept of the first year as *a critical period for learning*, a time when the trainee is uniquely ready to develop or change in the direction of the company's expectations.

They concluded that this pattern of increasingly challenging assignments followed by reinforcement was a key element in the development of successful managers, particularly during their first year when the organizational norms and expectations are set.

It seems clear that the initiating behaviors of the mentor—the demands, the challenges, the high expectations, and the confidence in the protégé—are precisely those behaviors which Berlew and Hall (as well as Moll and Rosenthal, cited earlier) have identified as critical in enhancing the probability of a person achieving his or her potential.

It might further be inferred that underlying the mentor's initiating behavior is a certain consciousness of the fact that if such a person as the prospective protégé—one he recognizes as an intelligent, well-educated, achievement-oriented person—is not "used" effectively, he or she will be literally and figuratively "wasted."

Whether or not this concern is initially motivated by altruism, intelligent self-interest, or organizational interests is irrelevant. The point is that the mentor acts on an intuitive evaluation and understanding of the person's needs. He provides a challenge which is sufficient to stimulate the motivation of the protégé, yet is within the present ability of the protégé to accomplish successfully.

Motivation

Earlier we asked the question: Why didn't these women perceive their mentors as oppressive tyrants or insatiable workaholics? Why were their sometimes unreasonable demands seen as challenging and motivating?

If we look back at the protégés' answers (on the foregoing pages), we see that being given meaningful work to do—work generally regarded as "man's work"—was a prime motivating force. The protégés viewed each successive level of challenge as an opportunity to further demonstrate their competence and to fulfill the expectations of their mentor. The intrinsic value of the work itself was enhanced by the implication of status and power associated with it and with the mentor. For these women, being given meaningful work to do by the professionally superior and powerful mentor was in and of itself motivation and reward. It was recognition of them as valuable organizational contributors and a reinforcement of their own sense of personal worth.

As noted earlier, if the mentor was perceived as an organizational "star," it is not difficult to see how the protégés may have envisioned themselves as "satellites" by association and identification.

McClelland's (1961) research on achievement motivation supports the protégés' interpretations of the mentors' behaviors and their responses to it. When achievement motivation is operating, he says, good performance becomes very attractive, as it was for these women. Moreover, this attractiveness is heightened by the process of identification—in this case the protégé's identification with the mentor.

McClelland also points out that achievement-oriented patterns of behavior are generally initiated very early in a person's life and are culturally bases. Depending upon child-rearing practices, he says, children coming from families where expectations for performance and independence are high, where parents evaluate accomplishments favorably and where the children are rewarded liberally, tend to develop into adults with strong achievement motivation and high self-esteem.

While gathering background data on the subjects' families was not part of this study, the interviews did reveal that most of the women came from families where expectations were high and achievement was valued. We might infer from this that the protégés were simply following preconditioned, well-established modes of behavior.

If we substitute the organizational environment for the biological family environment, then the mentor assumes the role of parent in the organizational context. If the analogy is followed through, the outcome predicted by McClelland—development of managers with strong achievement motivation and high self-esteem—is predictable.

chapter six

Total commitment: development

> Experience is not what happens to you; it is what you do with what happens to you.
> ALDOUS HUXLEY

The development stage, or Phase II of the mentor/protégé relationship, is just that: a period of development during which the patterns of behavior and response established in the initiation phase are built up, expanded and further reinforced. New behaviors are introduced as well.

Repeated Themes in the Behavior of Mentors

The principal mentor behaviors reported by the protégés as occurring during this development phase are described in Figure 4.

The following descriptions are representative of the first cluster of mentor behavior noted in Figure 4, i.e., an expansion of behaviors begun in the Initiation Phase. They are expressed in such a way that they often reveal some of the perceptions and feelings of the protégé as well.

contributed. I didn't say interfered: I said contributed to everybody's work in the whole department. So we all worked with him for whatever project we had underway. It was a team effort.

Teaching "tricks of the trade," the expansion of responsibilities, creating opportunities for the acquisition of new skills, together with critical feedback, serve to underscore the patterns of behavior begun in the Initiation Phase with regard to the work itself.

The following excerpts highlight the mentor's new behaviors and provide some clues as to his feelings toward his protégé:

> He almost always publicized my achievements and almost always gave me credit for them. And this was incredible.

> There is a regular program of exchange between the operating companies and the parent company. What happens is that the so-called "fast-trackers" or the ones with high potential are either requested or supplied by the home company or subsidiary to headquarters. What's called a rotational assignment. When he originally requested that I go down, I didn't want to. I fought the idea. But he convinced me it was right. And it was.

> I wanted to join (the top management group of a subsidiary). I felt it was a good opportunity for me. I was very disappointed that a young man was chosen out of here to go when I thought I should get that opportunity. He said, "It isn't the right thing for you right now. They'll chew you up down there." I said, "I don't care. I'm the most qualified person, and I want it." He said, "I know you are, but I don't think that in the long run it's the best thing for the company or for you." I was bitterly disappointed. As it turned out, it was a good thing. I came out much better. He was right.

> I can remember a mistake I made, an absolute disaster that I could still be horrified at right now. There was a voice on the phone screaming, "And who are you exactly to allocate expenses for my department?" He was a ferocious man, very large, very important in the scheme of things and very important to the president. I realized in a blinding flash I had no business doing this. But it was a great lesson and well-learned. He went storming into my boss's office looking for my head but my boss wasn't the slightest bit perturbed. I never made such a mistake again.

In this stage there appears to be a willingness on the part of the mentor to publicize not only the work of the protégé, but also his association with

	Frequency
• Teaches protégé the "tricks of the trade."	(9)
• Gives protégé all the responsibility she can handle (professional as well as personal).	(8)
• Thrusts protégé into areas for which she has no apparent experience or expertise.	(7)
• Directs and shapes through critical questioning.	(8)
• Publicizes protégé's achievements.	(7)
• Promotes steadily and often (or suggests that this be done, usually from above).	(7)
• Protects.	(6)

FIGURE 4. Repeated Themes in the Behavior of Mentors: Development, Phase II.

I learned what advertising is all about. There were a lot of little tricks about making sentences interesting and paragraphs readable. One of the most important things I learned was that when you're writing an advertisement, you're talking to somebody and that advertising should be written the way people talk—simply and as clearly as people talk to each other—unpretentiously avoiding all jargon of advertising, being emotional and warm, the way I would be when I'm talking to a friend.

He didn't limit my work. I was a secretary, but he didn't limit my work to shorthand and typing. That's the important thing. He gave me all I could handle, not just business things, but personal things as well. I'd help him look after his stock portfolio, for example. It was just another evidence of trust.

He was constantly moving me into new and untried situations. He started me talking to contemporaries. I can remember talking to a university class. And then I moved on from there to other groups. If he couldn't take a speaking engagement, I went in his place, which was not a natural thing for me. It was marvelous experience because I was doing things that women weren't doing at that time.

If we were doing a report on something, we might do it seven times through as he went through it piecemeal and said, "No, that's wrong. Change that. What does this mean? Go out and do some more work on it." So in the end when we got it done, it was perfect—as perfect as we knew how to make it. There was no question that it was perfect, because he turned it in. I should explain: he was then a man who knew everything that was happening in his department and her. Her achievements are now rewarded with the more commonly identified forms of reinforcement, promotion, recognition, etc. The most important new development in this stage, however, is the mentor's apparent willingness to shield the protege from unreasonable or unwarranted attack by other supervisors and/or co-workers, even at the risk of incurring their displeasure. He is willing also to risk her anger and a possible schism in their relationship to protect her from a perceived threat to her ultimate well-being.

The main concern here appears to be not so much the potential damage to her career progression—though that is an important consideration—but rather the potential damage to her ego.

Some tentative conclusions can be drawn from these behaviors about the mentor's feelings toward his protégé at this juncture—feelings of pride, certainly, as well as caring. For the sake of argument, one might view pride in a subordinate's accomplishments as purely self-enhancing and self-serving behavior. On the other hand, when the mentor's pride in the protégé's accomplishments is paired with a desire to shield and protect her, even at risk to himself, it seems reasonable to assume a depth of genuine feeling, a sense of caring beyond self-interest.

In summary, then, the behaviors of the mentor in the Developmental Stage fall into two categories: old behaviors that continue to expand on standards of performance, strengthen existing skills, and precipitate and encourage participation in a broader base of interests and experience; and new behaviors—publicizing, promoting and protecting—which seem to have less to do with the functional aspects of the job and more to do with a deepening emotional commitment and maintenance of the relationship. This dichotomy of behaviors—old and new, functional and emotional—will be reflected in the protégé's perceptions which follow.

Repeated Themes in the Protégés' Perception of Mentors' Behavior

As the protégés grow in experience and stature, they are aware of the mentors' efforts to expand their horizons and areas of expertise, though their motivations for doing so remain obscure. Most of the women said that they personally had no career goals that they were aware of, and that they didn't believe that their mentor had any "grand design" for them, either. Yet, they are very clear and articulate about the effect of the mentors' behaviors on their career development and its impact on their professional self-image at this stage. (See Figure 5.)

	Frequency
• Opportunities to gain broader experience or to improve in a particular dimension.	(10)
• Challenged to think more clearly and creatively.	(8)
• Opinions and points of view heard and valued even when they differ significantly from the mentor's.	(10)
• Free to make mistakes without fear.	(7)
• Progress based on professional performance.	(10)

FIGURE 5. Protégés' Perceptions of Mentors' Behavior: Development, Phase 11.

Once again, as in the Initiation Phase, demands are seen as opportunities, and forays into the unknown are termed "wonderful" and "challenging." the protégés' own accounts illustrate these points best:

> He had another great quality which I think was wonderfully helpful. He would talk things over with me—the problems he was facing in his own job—and say, "Would you like to put some thoughts together on such and such," or "What are we to do about this?" These might be things totally unrelated to my area of responsibility. For example, a special assignment. You know, he'd say, "Just drop everything and go to work on a plan to subcontract our engines to Chrysler." Things like that, which were totally outside of my experience.

It is worth noting that it was outstanding performance during just such "special assignments" that gave a number of the women, including the one just quoted, the diversity of experience needed to make them realistic candidates for the vice-presidential posts they now hold. Moreover, they were encouraged by their mentors to look beyond the specific to capture the "big picture" or to consider the strategic implications of what they were doing. This was accomplished in a variety of ways not altogether clear:

I think he challenged me to think more clearly and creatively. It was the sort of thing that, you know, he would just say a few words. Then, I'd say, "Yes, perhaps if I look at it from that point of view it might work better." They were not directives, they were just—he just dropped little seeds, you know, things that began to germinate. You'd think about them and come back with another alternative. Maybe he would suggest something else that would make you think about it a little more deeply still.

If I came to see him on an official visit, he would often use that opportunity to say, "Take a few minutes if you're not in a hurry. Tell me about what you're doing now. What are some of your thoughts about what is going on? What are your perceptions of what's happening within the company?" I had the sense that he must in some way value my opinion or he wouldn't be asking.

I made some spectacular errors, which I can remember very well; but he was not the kind of man who would ever say, "My God, that's wrong. Out!" So I was able to make mistakes.

How did the protégés know when they had gained stature? Certainly no bell tolled to mark the occasion, nor was there necessarily a prestigious appointment or a substantial increase in salary. The transition, though unheralded, was nonetheless distinct. They knew that they had "arrived" when they could express their own opinions freely and challenge their mentor's point of view without fear.

One protégé describes just that point in the relationship vividly:

The more I learned, the braver I got. The fact that most of what I learned, I learned from him didn't prevent disagreements from happening. Yes, we had big arguments. I wish there was some easy way to categorize them. They nearly always had to do with risk and always short-term risk. We never disagreed about anything long-term or what you might call the "big idea," but in how to execute things in the short term. Yes, indeed, big disagreements (smiling all the while). They were never really unpleasant and I rarely won. Once in a while, yes, once in a while I would prevail. He would let me make the mistake, or even be right.

Further confirmation of their stature and professional competence came as they began to climb the corporate ladder and compare themselves with organizational peers. ("Peers" here is used as a relative term because they had no peers, strictly speaking.)

I was promoted on a fairly frequent, and for this company, rapid basis. I moved ahead at the same pace as males. There were a number of us who came in at the same time, in the same year, and I either moved at the same pace or sometimes a little ahead of them. So I never had any sense that I wasn't being rewarded for what I was doing.... He was, for whatever reason, ahead of his time in his willingness to advance women.

Taken as a gestalt, then, the foregoing excerpts of the protégés' perceptions of the mentors' behaviors during the Development Phase, and the behaviors themselves, create an environment in which the protégés continue to be stretched and challenged by what seem at times unreasonable demands. Yet, the significant point here is that they were not simultaneously unreasonably constrained by their mentors. It is this relative lack of constraints that gives balance to the relationship and makes for growth.

This sense of balance in the relationship at this stage—plus and minus—is reflected also in the feelings engendered during this period of growth.

Repeated Themes in the Feelings Expressed by Protégés

As the relationship between mentor and protege grows more complex, feelings become more complicated too. Emotions are mixed. Positive sentiments continue to grow, while at the same time negative feelings begin to assert themselves. The emotional themes repeated most are described in Figure 6.

	Frequency
• Feelings aroused in Phase I reinforced.	(10)
• Feeling secure and/or supported.	(8)
• Feelings of isolation.	(8)
• Feelings of resentment.	(6)

FIGURE 6. Repeated Themes in the Feelings of Protégés: Development, Phase 11.

The feelings of gratitude, admiration and respect engendered in the Initiation Phase deepen and become much more personal, as the following comments suggest:

> It (the relationship) has been one of the greatest pleasures of my life. We can talk about anything and everything. We understand each other without going into a whole bunch of background. And we trust each other implicitly.
>
> I've always felt very close to him as an individual, as a person. That's been one of the most rewarding things for me. I have a great deal of respect for him.

It is clear from the foregoing that the relationship with the mentor has taken on a unique character for these protégés. The relationship has become a reward in itself. The closeness, the caring, the implicit trust all suggest the development of a love relationship. (The reference here is to an asexual love relationship.)

Important also is the sense of security and support the protégés feel. One protégé describes the sense of freedom such support provides:

> He is the kind of person that I feel I could talk to about anything. I could say how I truly felt. I wouldn't have to worry that I was overstepping in any way whatsoever. He is the only one I can really say that about honestly. I always felt I could say what I wanted to say without feeling that I was going to suffer as a consequence. And I was always very vocal.

As idyllic as the relationship appears to be from this preponderance of positive sentiments expressed, feelings of isolation, resentment and frustration are also experienced as this stage.

> They (associates) didn't like me too well. I think to some extent it was warranted. I fought very hard for what I wanted to do and what I thought was right to do. Sometimes I maybe hurt others a little bit, but I did it anyway. There was a little jealousy involved too because I did get a great deal of support from him. I was able to accomplish the things that I felt were important. He sponsored the things I wanted to do. Sometimes they were not popular with the others, and I sensed that they felt I was getting support I didn't deserve, but I thought I did deserve it. I gave up something in the way of friendships along the way, but the satisfaction I felt and the support I got from him made it all worthwhile.

The social isolation experienced by many of the women was not just inside the organization, but extended beyond working hours. As a group they did not socialize with colleagues—not even with the mentor—at this stage.

They did not frequent the squash or tennis courts or the after-hours watering holes; nor were they likely to be invited to dinner parties at the homes of their corporate colleagues. All of their communications, therefore, all of their inter-organizational relationship-building was confined narrowly to task-relevant interactions. This is a tremendously limiting factor in professional development per se, and in the development of an organizational power base in particular.

As for resentment and frustration, nothing grated more than the fact that for a long time they were doing a "man's job" for a "woman's wage."

> I used to be furious about it. I understood it intellectually, but emotionally, it still grates. I was never well-paid. He had a very interesting rationale for this. Unfortunately, more truth than poetry. He said, "If I tell them at headquarters that I have a job opening at this level, they will instantly send out four candidates—any of whom, on paper, will look better than you. So instead, I'll put you in this low level, and they'll say, 'Oh, well, nobody will want that job. Let her have it.'" And that's what he did. And it is true. They would have sent out candidates from headquarters, and I would not have gotten the job because on paper I didn't appear to have the qualifications. I would have missed the opportunity. There were a lot of years though when I was very hungry, and very angry. At this point, I've caught up.

In almost every case the "catch-up" period referred to here came after affirmative action legislation forced employers to reassess what they meant by "qualified."

The foregoing behaviors, perceptions and feelings described as dominant in the Development Phase reinforce many of the patterns of behavior established in the Initiation Phase. The significant changes are emotional in character and reflect the sensitivity on the part of both mentor and protégé to the delicate balance on which the relationship turns. While the multiplicity of demands persists, there are increasingly fewer constraints. Where in the Initiation Phase the work itself was its own reward, at this stage the reward has become the relationship itself. Each is willing to risk and sacrifice for the other. The closeness, the caring, the implicit trust all suggest the development of a love relationship. (The issue of sexuality in a love relationship will be discussed separately in Chapter Nine.)

DEMANDS COUNTERBALANCED BY FREEDOM

It is clear from the behaviors, perceptions and feelings identified in both the Initiation and Development Phases that the mentor creates an environment in which the protégé continues to be stretched and challenged with what seem at times unreasonable demands upon time, energy, and capabilities. Yet it is not the demands in themselves that are important. The significant point is that these demands are made in the context of considerable personal freedom. It is this relative lack of constraints that gives balance to the relationship and contributes to growth. In addition, the development of trust supports this freedom of action.

The protégés are free to try new things, to be creative. They are free to voice their opinions, to disagree. They have access to people and information far beyond their level in the organizational hierarchy. They are free to operate to a great extent outside the organizational norms for people at their level of management.

Organizational Socialization

Perhaps a review of the general process of organizational socialization will help to illustrate the ways in which the socialization of these women parallels the general model, and more particularly, the influence of the mentor on the outcome.

The process of organizational socialization described by Schein (1965) includes learning and internalizing the value system, the norms and the required patterns of behavior prescribed by the particular organization. The process of change a manager undergoes to assimilate these norms and values generally follows the classic change procedure originally formulated by Kurt Lewin. It involves three phases: unfreezing—preparation to learn the new values and norms; freezing—learning the new values and norms; and finally, refreezing—essentially internalizing the new values and norms.

The unfreezing phase serves the function of detaching the person from his or her former values. Schein says "He must redefine himself in terms of the new role which is to be granted." The role conflict Schein refers to here is inherent in the process of organizational socialization for any individual, but it is complicated by societal role conflict when the manager being socialized is female. Given that the managerial model is male, an aspiring young woman may find herself in a double bind.

Those aggressive, independent, task-oriented behaviors which are associated with the male managerial model are likely to be regarded as aberrant behavior by other females in the organization. On the other hand, male colleagues, constrained by stereotypic expectations, may be alternately offended or intimidated by her. With either group, the outcome is likely to be the same: She is rejected by females because of her aberrant behavior, and she is rejected by males because of her sex. Thus, she finds herself isolated and unloved, as it were.

The isolation reported by the women in this study made some of their experiences in the unfreezing phase of the socialization process particularly trying. Some of the upending experiences of Sloane Fellows which Schein describes are matched by the experiences of these women: the tremendous overload of work assigned; the responsibility for projects for which they had little or no previous experience; the lack of rapport with colleagues who did not regard them as peers. All of these experiences were tremendously anxiety-provoking situations involving risk of failure, frustration, diminution of self-esteem and possible humiliation. One might well ask: How were these women able to sustain themselves through this difficult period? And what prompted them to persevere?

A popular defense to help initiates endure the often unpleasant organizational pressures during the unfreezing process is to form peer groups of novices to provide support and sustain motivation. For the women in this study, however, there were no real peers, either among the women or among the men. There was only the mentor.

It is important to note here that though peer groups whose norms support organizational norms facilitate the socialization process, most organizational theorists would agree that the example provided by key members of management are by far the most potent influences. So while it was the mentor who created many of these upending and anxiety-provoking experiences, significantly, it was also the mentor who provided the support, the encouragement, and the managerial success model with which the protégés identified. It was the mentors' professional values, attitudes and behaviors that the protégés emulated and eventually internalized. Moreover, it was the mentors' blessing that mediated their acceptance into the management ranks and subsequently their advancement.

But what motivated these women? We said earlier that they were achievement-oriented. But is that alone sufficient explanation for why they persevered in the face of the isolation and rejection they suffered?

Schein explains that the success of such uncomfortable socialization experiences depends upon two factors: (1) the initial motivation of the person upon entering the organization; and (2) the degree to which a new member can be held captive during the socialization period. If motivation is high, he says, a person will tolerate an inordinate amount of pain to prove himself or herself worthy.

Just consider what it was the mentor offered to these women: He offered the opportunity to be regarded as someone "special"—intelligent, competent, valuable—someone respected as he was. It is hard to imagine today how unlikely such an opportunity was for a young woman in an organization only 25 short years ago.

As for being held captive during the socialization process, these women were literally held captive throughout most of their careers. Where else would they have gone? Even with the educational credentials they had, their real options for growth and advancement were few. Unlike the management skills of men, the management skills of women were not regarded as transferable from one organization to another. It was not until the affirmative action legislation of the early '70s that serious evaluation of female managers made organizational mobility a viable option.

Therefore, while these women suffered the pains of isolation and rejection for want of a peer group, they gained immeasurably from their close association with the mentor. The protégés' intuitive appreciation for the personal cost as well as the personal value of this trade-off may well account for the intensity of feeling which developed in these relationships between mentor and protégé.

Let us now look at what Schein describes as the basic responses to the dilemmas and conflicts of the organizational socialization process and see how they compare with the experience of the women in this study.

Basic Responses to Socialization

Type 1 - Rebellion	Rejection of all values and norms
Type 2 - Creative Individualism	Acceptance of only pivotal values and norms; rejection of all others
Type 3 - Conformity	Acceptance of all values and norms

Both Type 1 and Type 3 can be viewed as organizational failures, he says. Aspiring young men and women who persist in a belligerent and rebellious attitude toward organizational norms are likely to be expelled. Similarly, overly conforming men and women are likely to suppress their creativity, thus reducing their potential utility to the organization.

According to Schein's schema, those who really "succeed" in the process of organizational socialization to become viable candidates for top management are Type 2's. Clearly, the women in this study fit into this category. They represent those creative individuals who somehow manage to maintain their own integrity throughout the process, accepting only those organizational norms and values which are pivotal to the specific requirements of the job, and rejecting all those which are inconsistent with their personal and professional values.

Remaining creatively individualistic in an organization through various levels of management can be very difficult for both men and women as resocialization takes place at each level. But it was particularly difficult for the women in this study, for the reasons noted earlier. With each move, they had to start all over again—not only being the new person in the group, but once more being the only woman in the group.

Throughout the process of organizational socialization, the one consistent, stabilizing and guiding influence was the influence of the mentor. It seems unlikely that these women would have been able to resist the overwhelming forces toward conformity and become the creative individuals they did become without the tutelage, reinforcement and protection of their mentors.

- Recommends protégé to top management
  (usually to the parent company or to the board
  of directors). (9)
- Lets go. (10)

FIGURE 7. Repeated Themes in the behavior of Mentors: Termination, Phase III.

The protégés' comments, in retrospect, suggest that the knowledge acquired from the mentor, even by osmosis, had the effect of focusing and strengthening their own inclinations and shaping their behavior.

The following excerpts underscore this point:

> I think one of the main things that I learned from him was to set extremely high standards for myself, to never hesitate to go deeper into a project, and to trust my own intuition. Now this is something you won't hear from him because he has made a name as being someone who tests everything—researches everything. But, boy, I think that nine-tenths of what he has contributed were purely great leaps of intuition. I couldn't watch this and not learn that if a person were gifted with any intuition at all, that you had to rely on it. And I think that what has helped me more than anything else is a belief in what I intuitively feel is the correct answer and to be able to recognize it. So that when it's there, I don't think things through to the point where you make mincemeat of it or mash it up.

> I worked very closely with him and he had, when something really went sour, he had the ability to be optimistic. To say, "Well, there are other fish to fry. There are other ways of solving this problem. There are other accounts out there." He didn't stew in his own misery, which I think many people, including me, have a tendency to do.

> He had this down to a fine point. He never lost his cool, never. I never saw him. He was never impolite. The control that man exerted over himself was unbelievable. People might say things that were outrageous or he'd feel that his rights were being invaded. And he would say, "Gentlemen, I really need your counsel, you're creating a terrible problem for me." Then he would go on and say, "You are proposing to do thus and so, and of course, our charter is this, and you're really giving away free what I was charged for. Now, how would you suggest I handle that?" Then all of a sudden all the steam would go out of the steamroller. He just was super at it.

Many of the attitudes and values, as well as the professional style, of the mentor have been internalized by the protégé by the time the Termination

chapter seven

Infinite closeness: termination

> The true virtue of human beings is fitness to live together as equals;... and preferring whenever possible the society of those with whom leading can be alternate and reciprocal.
> JOHN STUART MILL

The mentor/protégé relationship during this termination phase progresses of its own momentum, without the impetus of many new or specific behaviors. The development is subtle and the changes are situationally induced.

Repeated Themes in the Behavior of Mentors

The most pronounced themes of the mentors' behavior which emerge during this stage are shown in Figure 7.

Frequency

- Provides opportunities to learn by osmosis, observation, and association.   (10)

Stage is reached. Mentor behaviors, in the developmental sense, are no longer overt, and the protégé's response (learning) is not necessarily conscious at the time.

Change in the relationship, at this stage, is largely a function of organizational change:

> When it was established that he was going to replace the corporate president, it was clear he could no longer handle being president of the subsidiary as well. He asked me to take it over.
>
> When he became president and chief executive officer, I became his assistant and later vice president.

This same scenario—in which the protégé steps into the mentor's shoes or becomes his vice-presidential assistant—is repeated in a number of cases, but not without some difficulty. As the women themselves pointed out, without the impetus of affirmative action legislation, it seems unlikely that many of their appointments to presidential and vice-presidential posts would have been confirmed, however competent they may have been. In one instance, the board refused to accept the mentor's recommendation that his protégé replace him. The company went through two male replacements before they finally appointed her—his hand-picked and trained protégé—to the responsible and prestigious position. She has since built upon her mentor's performance and surpassed it. The fact that they, mentor and former protégé, remain devoted friends says something powerful and beautiful about the relationship and the stature of the individuals.

It is the acknowledgment that they are peers, and the mentor's effectively "letting go" that signal the termination of the mentor/protégé relationship and the possible commencement of a compeer relationship.

One of the mentors verbalized the psychological act of letting go when his protégé took on the presidency of a major subsidiary. Said he: "Now you are on your own. You are it!"

Of course, the actual letting go was much more gradual and the need to be in touch very real, as this excerpt makes clear:

> What I do and what he does are no longer directly interrelated, but we stay very much in touch. We have long luncheons together now. Usually, mostly I listen. I don't talk that much; I just listen to him. We talk as friends, long-time acquaintances. We talk about business in general, about what's going on in the world. I have a lot of international business and certainly he can provide a financial perspec-

tive—but not the day-to-day operational perspective that I have in those countries. He is a very exciting man, even today; and he's past 60.

The mentor now becomes a resource person, a trusted friend and counselor with whom you might clear your thinking, sound out the validity of an important decision. He is a person whom you trust to have your best interests at heart, someone who would risk telling you what you need to know even though it might be painful to you. He is someone whose perspective and judgment you value and trust implicitly.

The changing nature of the relationship during the Termination Phase is reflected in the protégés' perceptions and feelings as well.

Repeated Themes in the Protégés' Perceptions of Mentors' Behavior

At this advanced stage of the relationship, the protégé's image of herself vis a vis her mentor comes into sharp focus and more closely resembles the current reality.

The dominant themes in the protégés' perceptions of the mentors' behaviors reflect this perceptual adjustment, as shown in Figure 8.

Frequency

- Awareness of one's own special strengths and contributions to the relationship. (7)
- Fallibility of the mentor recognized. (7)

FIGURE 8. Repeated Themes in the Protégés' Perception of Mentors' Behavior: Termination, Phase 111.

While the protégés are very much aware of their own special strengths, they are also very protective of their mentor's image. They continue to refer to him with a certain deference. However, it is clear, at least in the minds of the protégés, that the relationship has been redefined, as the following excerpts illustrate:

> I knew it had ended when—there are certain areas in which he is much better than I am and always will be. There will never be anybody who understands print advertising as well as he does. He is good in television, but I don't think his instincts are as good about it

as mine are. It is a different discipline. It's not a discipline the way that print is, and I suppose it ended at the point where I was able to contribute, I think, different things to our work because of the medium in which I was working than he was able to.... He wouldn't agree with this, incidentally. I'm sure he'd hate me saying this. But I think deep down he might acknowledge its truth.

Our relationship has changed because he is a little bit weaker (emotionally) than he appeared to be before. He has become more human—less all-knowing—more a personal friend and less a professional sponsor.

Though disappointed and often frustrated for want of legitimate power and recognition during the Development Stage, the protégés in this Termination Stage seem incredibly sensitive to and understanding of the tremendous personal and societal pressures by which their mentors were constrained.

On being passed over for the top slot several times:

He made some moves which I think even he would admit today were not good moves. He put some people in charge who were more expedient than right, and so I ... he just was not ready at the time to support a woman to the exclusion of all else.

He has a great many hangups about women in business. There were points at which he couldn't overcome these hangups. Let's just say there were problems along the route. I'm not saying that this was a totally open man to a woman in business. But he did the best he could given his background, and I think he overcame a lot of emotional hesitation in order to do these things. He certainly did a lot more than most men in similar positions were doing at the time so I can't fault him for not being perfect.

It seems reasonable to ask: Had the protégés been men, would their resentment have been greater? Different perhaps, along oedipal lines? Would it have resulted in bitter feelings and confrontation? Would the relationship have been terminated?

In considering these questions it might be helpful to bear in mind the societal context within which these relationships developed and the realities of organizational life at the time. (More on this in the next chapter.) While their achievements were acknowledged in their respective organizations, in contrast to their male peers in top management, their competence was not perceived as transferable to other organizational contexts at the same level. In other words, they had no viable alternative.

Though not perfect, the world created by their mentors was the best of worlds available to them and the protégés knew it. The relative position of these women vis à vis their male counterparts and their relative status in the business community as a whole may account for much of the stability characteristic of these mentor/protégé relationships. The feelings expressed by the protégés in the next section will support this notion.

Repeated Themes in the Protégés' Emotional Response

The feelings expressed by the protégés as the functional aspects of the relationship wind down reveal women who have come of age—not just professionally, but emotionally as well.

The most dominant feelings expressed by the protégés during the Termination Stage are shown in Figure 9.

Frequency

- Pride in achievement. (10)
- Infinite closeness. (9)

FIGURE 9. Repeated Themes in Protégés' Emotional Response: Termination, Phase 111.

The protégés during this stage feel independent and self-confident and exhibit a real sense of pride in their achievements:

> It was my burning ambition to become a vice-president of the parent company because no woman had ever been. I was the first woman to accomplish that and I am still the only one. (She is the highest-ranking woman in the industry.)
>
> I'm here to tell you I have direct line responsibility for a company with 300 million in assets, and the bottom line—black or red—makes a big difference.
>
> He (the mentor) is the president of a company, and I'm not, but probably in general peer terms, we have been on a level for several years. But I probably make more money than he does now, and I have a job, well . . . " (In this case as well, she is the highest-ranking woman in the respective industry.)

Significantly, in assessing their accomplishments, these women are neither arrogant nor self-effacing. But they are careful to differentiate themselves from women who have recently been named to vice-presidential positions in the areas of consumer affairs, equal opportunity and the like. Not that they regard these as unimportant functions; they simply feel that these positions are not analogous to their own functions. In other words, they are not top management jobs; they are not decision-making functions. As one woman put it, "Those are just dress-up titles."

So, while it is clear from the feelings expressed by the protégés that they are self-sufficient now, in every case they still maintain close and affectionate ties with the mentor. Feelings of infinite closeness are expressed:

> While the relationship has changed in nature, it still retains its richness.
>
> We became friends during the time he was my boss, and we will be friends until one of us dies.

The depth of emotion characteristic of the true mentor/protégé relationship is summed up beautifully by one of the women. After reciting a litany of her mentor's singular abilities and accomplishments, the protégé was asked what her feelings for her mentor were now, some ten years later. She replied simply: "Just short of adoring!"

Perhaps it is a misnomer, then, to call this phase of the relationship the Termination Phase, because in truth, it never really ends. The relationship changes during this phase in the sense that there is no longer direct task-relevant interaction and direct influence between mentor and protégé. The values, the attitudes, the skills, the professional style of the mentor have been selectively internalized by the protégé. She has become a success in her own right. She has outgrown the need for his tutelage. However, the need for the relationship continues. The need for contact with the mentor, the need to share experiences—even the need for approval—persist. The feelings of love endure.

FUNCTIONAL PROXIMITY BECOMES INFINITE CLOSENESS

During all three stages of the mentoring process, a richness of rapport, a caring, a trust develops between mentor and protégé which can be described as a love relationship. Let us examine once more what is happening from the protégé's perspective and see what that tells us about the relationship.

Feelings of gratitude, admiration and enhanced self-image in the early stage of the relationship deepen as the relationship develops. The respect, trust and love which grows between the pair in the Development Phase is an outgrowth of many, many interactions, trials and tests which were described in detail in Chapter Six.

However, it is important to appreciate the fact that the relationship is not conflict-free. Feelings of isolation and resentment on the part of the protégé are alternately confronted, resolved or rationalized. Similarly, sexual tensions (to be discussed in the next chapter) are finessed, rationalized or denied. It is the ability of mentor and protégé to confront one another on issues and yet maintain their respect and affection for one another that tests the real strength of the relationship and the participants. Ultimately, the protégé is no longer dependent upon the mentor's tutelage; but their respective needs for contact, approval and love continue.

The feelings shared by mentor and protégé, then, are not merely feelings of respect and admiration for a person's professional competence. Rather they are an expression of complete confidence in the essential "goodness" of the person as a human being. There is complete trust. Mentor and protégé are willing to render themselves vulnerable to one another.

Clearly, there is tremendous risk in such a relationship. As Daniel Levinson points out: "There is plenty of room for exploitation, undercutting, envy, smothering, and oppressive control on the part of the mentor, and for greedy demanding, clinging admiration, self-denying gratitude, and arrogant ingratitude on the part of the recipient."

But there is also a tremendous opportunity for professional and emotional growth—for both mentor and protégé. To quote Carl Rogers (1958): "The degree to which I can create relationships which facilitate the growth of others as separate persons is a measure of the growth I have achieved myself."

In his analysis of constructive relationships, Rogers emphasizes the quality of the relationship as a whole, not just the short-run tactics of "human relations." He suggests that the most important messages in a relationship are communicated not by words but by a multitude of subliminal signals that convey the speaker's true attitudes. These subliminal signals are the substance of the protégés' perceptions of the mentors' behavior and vice versa.

What seems to be important to the influencee, says Rogers, is whether the influencer accepts him as a person and is engaging in a genuine relationship. He avoids engaging in what may appear to be manipulative strategies. In other words, both parties need to feel that there is an accurate matching of their experience, awareness and communication with one another. In Rogers' terms, they are experiencing "congruence" in their relationship. This, says Rogers, is of central importance in the development of growth-facilitating relations.

The degree of honesty and emotional maturity required to maintain such an intimate relationship poses serious problems for many. As Rogers explains, the participants in such a relationship are frequently faced with the existential choice:

> Do I dare to communicate the full degree of congruence which I feel? Do I dare match my experience, and awareness of that experience, with my communication? Do I dare to communicate myself as I am or must my communication be somewhat less than or different from this? The sharpness of this issue lies in the often vividly foreseen possibility of threat or rejection. To communicate one's full awareness of the relevant experience is a risk in interpersonal relationships. It seems to me that *it is the taking or not taking of this risk which determines whether a given relationship becomes more and more mutually therapeutic or whether it leads in a disintegrative direction.* (emphasis added)

Letting Go

There comes a time in mentoring relationships, as in other constructive relationships, such as those between teacher and student, supervisor and subordinate, parent and child, when mentor and protégé must quite literally let go of one another if the relationship is to continue to grow. This sounds incongruous, but it is not. Without overdramatizing the importance of disengagement in a mentoring relationship, consider the following analogy.

When a child is ready to be born, it must leave the safety of the mother's womb or both parent and child will surely perish. They may die or suffer serious impairment in the process of birth, but the probability of survival and growth for both is infinitely greater. The longer the separation is delayed, the greater the risk of death. There is an appropriate time for disengagement in a mentoring relationship, and both mentor and protege know it intuitively. However, mentor and protégé often develop such a strong dependence upon one another—a dependence either real or imagined—that the prospect of change in the relationship is viewed as a threat. They resist facing the inevitable. As a consequence, the longer the inevitable is delayed, the greater the risk of dissolution and/or disenchantment.

In summary, then, the degree to which mentor and protégé are prepared to take risks with one another—beyond their professional role expectations—will determine the constructive or destructive direction of the relationship.

chapter eight

Mentoring relationships gone awry

> It is not true that suffering ennobles the character; happiness does that sometimes, but suffering for the most part makes men petty and vindictive.
> SOMERSET MAUGHAM

The purpose of this chapter is to analyze the interviews of women who claimed not to have had any significant supportive relationships in their careers. We will first attempt to determine if there was any significant difference in their profiles, in terms of title, career progression, education, average number of years with the company, salary, age and marital status. Second, we will look into the question of how, if indeed they had no supportive relationships, they were able to meet their needs for support, direction and identification.

THE NON-MENTOR GROUP

Profile

Of the survey sample of 35 women, only five reported having had no significant professional relationship. In very general terms, their profiles are not unlike the profiles of the women in the mentor group. They are well-educated, achievement-oriented and successful businesswomen. The differences are subtle and pose some interesting questions. Let us look first at the comparison of the profiles of the mentor and non-mentor group which appears in Table 8-1.

TABLE 8.1. Comparison of Mentor and Non-Mentor Group

	Mentor	Non-mentor
Title: At least Vice President	100%	60%
Career progression: staff	90%	100%
Education: graduate degree	60%	60%
Average number of years with company	22 years	8.5 years
Salary: over $50,000	80%	20%
Average age	50 years	38 years
Married	50%	20%

Only three, or 60 percent of the non-mentor group, have as yet reached the vice-presidential level; and only one earns more than $50,000 a year, although educationally they are as well-prepared for their careers as are the women in the mentor group.

The average age of the non-mentor group, however, is 38, as opposed to 50 for the mentor group. So we might conclude that given another ten years the profiles of the mentor and non-mentor group will match with respect to title and salary, as they do now in terms of education and career progression. But there is another important factor to consider that is not immediately apparent from a glance at Table 8.1. The difference in the average number of years with the company is not so much a function of differences in the ages of the women in the mentor and non-mentor groups as it is a function of differing career patterns. The women in the non-mentor group, with one exception, have had more company moves than the women in the mentor group. In addition, all expressed varying degrees of dissatisfaction with their progress and/or experiences in these companies.

It is interesting and significant that the profile of the non-mentor sample of women in this study—however small—bears a striking resemblance to the non-mentor group of men in the Heidrick & Struggles survey discussed in Chapters One and Three. That is, in general, in the non-mentor groups both men and women earned less, moved more, and were less satisfied with their lot.

The most striking finding from our point of view, however, is that the women in the non-mentor group *did* in fact have mentors or sponsors whom they did not recognize or chose to deny. During the interviews a number of personal life traumas were revealed which might offer a possible explanation for the need these women apparently felt to deny supportive relationships which were clearly there and which the women themselves described.

Unrecognized and Unacknowledged Mentors

During one interview, the subject described three intimate supportive relationships with top executives, but she discounted them because they were outside her own organization. She had read some of the popular literature about "corporate godfathers," and jumped to the conclusion that supportive relationships outside the organization didn't count. So, she reported "none" in answer to the survey question: "Is there some one person (or perhaps more than one person) who stands out in your mind as the one who *most* influenced your career development at a critical juncture (perhaps a boss, a senior staff person, a teacher, a consultant who helped you to acquire the professional skill and sophistication required to advance to higher corporate levels)?" It is worth noting that the wording of the question does not limit the answer to people inside the organization.

The subsequent interview revealed, however, that it was the close interaction with these three corporate executives, whom she referred to as her "Dutch Uncles," which provided her with much of the cultural know-how and decision-making perspective that she used to her advantage in advancing her career in her own organization. In fact, one of the relationships with a CEO developed along much the same lines as the mentor/protégé relationships outlined in Chapter Four. The major difference is that in this case the mentor was not the one who promoted the protégé within the organization, though he contributed significantly to her promotability.

Moreover, their emotional involvement developed along sexual lines. Perhaps because the mentor was outside the organization and because mentor and protégé were both free, they did not have to deal with the sexual tensions experienced in those mentor/protégé relationships constrained by prior commitments and organizational norms.

In yet another case both mentor and protégé were top managers in the same company. Their relationship developed along sexual lines as well, and this aspect of the relationship became a detriment to their career advancement. Both mentor and protégé were forced to resign their positions. The organizational norms would not support such an alliance, even though the participants divorced their respective spouses and married one another. One might argue that the affair was a "red herring" and there were organizational forces afoot to discredit either one or both of the participants. Even if that were true (and the researcher has a sense that it is true), the validity of the argument doesn't change the predictability of the outcome.

However much we may think societal views on intimate sexual relationships have changed, many of the old taboos persist. When one has moved to the top of the organizational hierarchy—particularly if the ascent was swift—there are bound to be those who are resentful or at the very least envious. Where these individuals would be reluctant to discredit an outstanding performer, even in their own minds, they may self-righteously condemn an indiscretion by a corporate officer, male or female, in the name of organizational image.

Since this interview took place shortly after this traumatic experience, it is not surprising that this woman denied having had help from anyone *ever*.

In yet another case, husband and wife entered the organization together. She advanced much more rapidly than he and eventually became his boss. She is now the top-ranking woman in the company. They are divorced. Both continue to work in the same company.

"Far and away," she says, "it has been the most challenging managerial problem I have ever had."

This woman described in detail the man who "discovered her," gave her a job, sponsored her with a scholarship to go to college and provided her with career direction. Yet, she did not perceive this supportive relationship as significant to her career. Her perspective was narrowly confined to the present and the organization. It seems that the person from whom she needed and sought support, her husband, did not provide it. Similarly, when she asked for counsel from her supervisors, they refused to "get involved." It is conceivable that the rift between husband and wife made other possible supporters hesitant to assume the role of arbitrator or benefactor. She described herself as essentially a "loner" and isolated in the organization.

These women all claimed: "No one ever helped me." "Whatever I have accomplished, I did it myself." "I've never had anyone shepherd me along."

The pattern of denial is clear. These women who claim not to have had any mentors or sponsors did in fact have them. They simply did not recognize them as such, or for their own reasons chose to deny them. So in profile at least, even with respect to actually having had a mentor, the mentor and non-mentor groups appear to be identical.

PERCEPTUAL DIFFERENCE BETWEEN MENTOR AND NON-MENTOR GROUPS

Was there something revealed by the interviews that somehow distinguishes these two groups of women from one another? Yes, indeed there is: Their perceptions of the world are antithetical.

The non-mentor group perceives the world as hostile and threatening—a place where their real worth is not valued and they have had to fight for everything they have ever gotten. They feel denied and unloved, and they continue to support their view of the world by effectively screening out help and support, as these excerpts suggest:

"I sort of look around and laugh to myself when you ask about support, because I really, very seldom *notice* support."

The researcher sensed a bitterness, a hostility and a discontent in the demeanor of these women which was in sharp contrast to the mentor group. Significantly, they are perceived differently by their colleagues as well. Generally, they are perceived as "cold and emotionally distant." One of the women says she was perceived by her subordinates as "cold and inhuman" when she was in a line position.

The women admit to being hurt and somewhat confused by this perception because they don't see themselves in this light. Yet they understand how it happens.

As one explains:

> "It is very true that at the top of my list was always performance. Get the job done. Don't spend time gossiping. Get on with it. But it still hurts."

While the mentor group also stressed performance and experienced feelings of isolation, their behavior was mitigated by their perception of the world.

The mentor group views the world as an exciting and challenging place where most people are well-intentioned, helpful and supportive. They see themselves in this light and are generally perceived so by their colleagues and subordinates. The following is a description of one of the mentor group by one of her subordinates, but it is representative of the style employed by the mentor group as a whole:

> "She has a unique ability to join the troops in the trenches, exhorting them at the same time she is planning the victory dinner." Explaining her motivational style, he adds, "She can make me believe I'm a cornerstone of the company."

It seems reasonable to infer from the foregoing that these two groups' antithetical perceptions of the world make a difference in the quality of their lives, and in the quality of the lives they touch.

The women who claim not to have had mentors were denied the kind of support and love they felt they needed, and perhaps as a consequence they now feel compelled to deny the support and even the love that they were given. In any event, it is clear that they have not yet come to terms with their anger and resentment.

The damage to these women personally is apparent, as the pain they felt and their latent hostility was communicated to the interviewer as they spoke. But if this hostility was communicated to the interviewer in a period of a few hours, is it not also communicated on a day-to-day basis to those whom they supervise and train for management? It seems probable that such hostility is communicated and perpetuated—though not consciously.

It is not our intent to overemphasize this point; however, one might consider the battered child syndrome in family life. If we can view the organization as a community—a family, if you will—and the mentor as a surrogate parent, then it is reasonable to presume that the loved child—the one with a mentor—becomes in turn a loving parent. Similarly, the ignored, abused and often battered child—the one denied the love of a mentor—becomes an indifferent and dispassionate parent at best.

When one considers that leadership succession is one of the principal responsibilities of top management, then the implications of this analogy are profound.

chapter nine

Agapē versus sex in mentoring relationships

> Love is an energy which exists of itself. It is its own value.
> THORNTON WILDER

The great Spanish phiosopher Jose' Ortega y Gasset once remarked that "for many years much has been said about love affairs and little about love." We presume that people know what we are talking about when we talk of love. But do they? Distinctions are varied, and often obscure.

In our culture, love and sex are inexorably linked. Men, and more recently women, have come to enjoy (and some to prefer) physical intimacy without emotional involvement. Sex without love is an accepted phenomenon, but the reverse is not true. Love without sex is suspect particularly between a man and a woman.

The Platonic relationship which the ancient Greeks considered the ideal of love was presumed to exist only between men. Women were somehow considered incapable of such emotional nobility, if indeed they were considered in this context. After all, a Platonic relationship is one in which there is a meeting of the minds. Implicit in such a relationship is the notion of equality of status and intellect—if not in the immediate present, most certainly in the future. The men engaged in Platonic relationships were the bright young sons of the noble class who were being carefully groomed by their tutors to fulfill their potential in society.

In this respect, the emotional intimacy which develops in a Platonic relationship is analogous to the emotional intimacy which develops between mentor and protégé. Mutual admiration, respect, shared experiences, shared dreams, and yes, love is engendered. But what kind of love?

The ancient Greeks thought of love as being divided into three broad categories: *agapē*, or spiritual love; *philia*, or familial love; and *eros*, romantic or sexual love. Clearly *agapē* was the ideal. To quote Plato : "This is that love which is of the heavenly goddess Aphrodite, and is heavenly, and of great price to individuals and to cities, making the lover and the beloved alike eager in the work of their own improvement."

The Greek word *agapē* was reserved for the highest order of love to which Plato refers—literally a sharing of charitable gifts. It represents a divine aspiration for knowledge and wisdom, which is then shared. The essence of *agapē* love is benevolence and grace.

One can better appreciate the purity of the sentiment which the word connotes when one realizes that *agapē* was the word used later in Christian theology to denote the sharing of Christ's love in the distribution of the Eucharist.

In contrast, *eros* was used to denote the sexual aspects of love—clearly a lower order. It was regarded as natural and even necessary, but hardly ennobling. To quote Plato once more: "Evil is the vulgar lover who loves the body rather than the soul." It is easy to see why *eros* was often referred to as the "dark passion," and the one most often associated with women.

While these concepts of love and sex are philosophical and theological in nature, they are the source from which our contemporary notions of love are drawn. They represent the beliefs upon which many of the current conventions which dictate the behaviors of men and women are based.

To a great extent the societal mind-set which perceives woman as a love/sex object to be acquired—as opposed to woman as a peer with whom love is shared—still persists.

SEXUAL TENSIONS BETWEEN MENTORS AND PROTÉGÉS

One of the many complexities of the mentoring relationship, then, is the sexual tension that develops between two people in such an intimate relationship, particularly when the two people are of the opposite sex.

When one works closely, as these women did, with men who are as brilliant, dynamic and often physically attractive as these mentors were perceived to be by their protégés, it would be extraordinary if sexual tension did not exist between the two. However, one needs to differentiate between pressure exerted to gain sexual favors and the strong emotional involvement that develops between mentor and protégé where sexual attraction may be one of many attractions the pair shares.

Since we are all sexual beings, the question then becomes: How is sexual tension dealt with in such an intimate relationship? This is not a question which lends itself to a generalized answer. The sexual tensions experienced by the women in this study were dealt with in ways which were tolerable and constructive for them—and the ways varied.

One protégé saw her mentor as the father she had lost in early childhood. She revealed the transference of her love in this way:

> "He (the mentor) is a person I idealize and love. If I could have had a father.... (voice trails off, eyes closed and speaking almost in a whisper)... and he is younger than I am. I don't know many other men I feel that way about."

They are both married. And while they do not socialize outside the office, they share their very special joys and sorrows with each other.

Conversely, a mentor felt it necessary to relate to his protégé as a daughter in order to maintain the appropriate psychological distance. (She was by far the most physically attractive woman interviewed.) This strategy worked well for both of them initially, but it became particularly frustrating for the protégé when she gave up thinking of him as a father figure. Her subsequent marriage buttressed the mentor's psychological barrier.

Another protégé, after describing her mentor in the most adoring terms and manner, dismissed the issue of sexual attraction between them in this way:

You don't have time. You just don't have time. There are a lot of attractive people around, very attractive people. And some of them are very exciting, inspiring people for a long time, and some of them are very exciting, inspiring people for half an hour. If you're an adult, you can deal with that. I think it is a pretty crummy cop-out for men and women who think it can't be dealt with, that it can't be walked away from. It's just about as hard as not eating a pastry if you really want to lose weight.

This flip and somewhat detached response belies the intensity of emotion exhibited by the protégé in answering the question. From the moment the issue of sexuality in the relationship was broached, the protégé became nervous and agitated and avoided the eyes of the interviewer as she spoke.

One possible conclusion is that the sexual tension between her and her former mentor—even now—is much more difficult to deal with than passing up an eclair.

Though they no longer work together in the same organization, they continue to see each other as close friends.

Then there are those situations in which there is love on both sides, but only one party is sexually aroused. One mentor comforted his protégé through the rocky first years of her marriage. Later, she comforted him through his divorce. While she cared deeply for him, she was totally unprepared to risk a now stable marriage to fill the void in her mentor's life. It was a painful transition, but their ability to communicate openly with one another about their feelings made it possible to talk it through and salvage a meaningful relationship. She and her husband hosted the reception when the now-former mentor subsequently remarried.

Another variation of the foregoing situation is when one or both of the participants in a mentoring relationship is homosexual.

While the means used to deal with sexual tensions in the relationship seem varied, the basic strategy employed is the same: To distance oneself either psychologically or physically from the other person. Those who cast mentor or protégé in the role of father or daughter protect themselves from their desire by the taboos associated with incestuous relationships. Those who are still uncomfortable with their sexual feelings deny any serious stirrings of the flesh, and sublimate their desires by focusing all of their energies on professional achievement. And still others may marry to escape their strong attraction for the mentor and thus resolve their conflict in a personally and socially acceptable way.

One might presume that sexual intimacy between mentor and protégé might further enhance and strengthen an already rich relationship, but there was no evidence to support such a notion among the interviewees. All of the women who acknowledged having had a mentor felt that sexual intimacy with the mentor would have threatened the existing relationship, and they were not prepared to take that risk.

Summary

While all of the mentor/protégé relationships acknowledged in this study are still ongoing, it is reasonable to assume that if the participants had engaged in what were perceived as manipulative and/or exploitive behaviors, the relationships would have been aborted or truncated at some point along the way. In fact, some of the denied relationships of the non-mentor group may be examples of just such dysfunctional behavior and its consequences.

In the ideal, the mentor/protégé relationship is built upon a mutuality of trust and eventually unconditional love. While often frustrated and disappointed, the participants look to the overall quality of the relationship on balance. At every stage the quality of the relationship must outweigh the sum of its shortcomings in the minds of the participants. In the end, the relationship is maintained not because of what one member can do for the other, but because mentor and protégé truly care for one another. The relationship has value in and of itself.

chapter ten

An analysis of the mentoring phenomenon

> The degree to which I can create relationships which facilitate
> the growth of others as separate persons is the measure of
> the growth I have achieved myself.
> CARL ROGERS

At the outset of our investigation, a review of the existing literature on the topic of mentoring in general and mentoring in the organizational context in particular, was spare and provided little insight as to the nature of the process of mentoring. To be sure, there were descriptions, conceptions, bits and pieces, but nothing that could be described as a complete process applied to a specific and homogeneous group.

As a consequence of our analysis of the mentoring relationships of the top management women in this study, a dynamic process of mentoring has been described from beginning to end. Beyond this, our efforts to explain the phonemenon have led us to a number of conclusions as well as powerful theories and principles of human relationships from other disciplines. It is our sense that these conclusions, together with the cited theories and principles, are relevant to mentoring relationships in organizations, and may enhance our understanding of mentoring as a phenomenon.

WHAT IS A MENTOR?

Mentors have been referred to in the popular press variously as godfathers, coaches, rabbis, guides, teachers, counselors, and a host of other pseudonyms. There is however, no consensus on what the word really means, and Webster does not help much. The dictionary tells us simply that Mentor was the name of the teacher whom Odysseus entrusted with the education of his son, Telemachus, in Homer's Greek epic, *The Odyssey*.

Our analysis of the data suggests that these pseudonyms really represent *different* kinds of supportive relationships. It might be helpful, therefore, to think of supportive relationships along a continuum such as the one shown in Figure 10, representing increasing degrees of power.

Continuum of Supportive Relationships

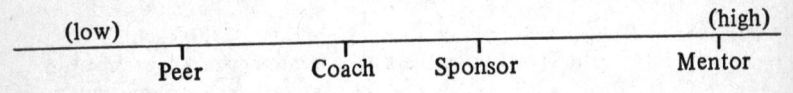

```
(low)                                               (high)
|------------|------------|------------|------------|
      Peer        Coach       Sponsor        Mentor
```

FIGURE 10. Degree of Power—Access to Resources of All Kinds, i.e., Expertise, Influence, Status, Time, Money, Information, etc. [Suggested by the conceptual model of Shapiro, Hazeltine & Rowe (1978)].

While a mentor can assume any one or all of the less powerful roles—sponsor, coach, even peer—the reverse is not true. Sponsors, coaches and peers, though developmentally significant, do not have the degree of influence mentors have upon their protégés.

Differences Between Mentors and Sponsors

The sponsor is a person who promotes, literally and figuratively. Sponsoring is an administrative function. The relationship is one of utility. There is little ego involvement. If the sponsorship should end, one would regret the loss of an important utility, but one's ego would be relatively mentors are loved. What can we say about the characteristic elements of these powerful and intense mentoring relationships?

Characteristic Elements of Mentoring Relationships

There are three elements which this research indicates distinguish *true* mentoring relationships (the highest point on the continuum in Figure 10) from other kinds of supportive relationships:

1. The *power* that the mentor represents in terms of access to resources of all kinds, personal and material, i.e., expertise, influence, status, time, money, information, etc. The mentor, in general, will possess or have access to more power than either a sponsor, a coach, or a peer.

2. The *level of identification* that develops between mentor and protégé, i.e., the degree to which the protege identifies with the mentor both in terms of professional values and behavior and in terms of personal values and behavior, will be greater between mentor and protégé than between any of the other dyads noted on the continuum of supportive relationships.

3. The *intensity of emotional involvement*, i.e., the psychological bonding, the linking of minds, the sharing of dreams, and the eventual sharing of unconditional love, occurs *only* in true mentoring relationships. It is significantly absent in sponsoring relationships.

FIGURE 11. Levels of Power, Identification, and Emotion.

CHARACTERISTIC ELEMENTS OF MENTORING RELATIONSHIPS

Elements	Phase I	Phase II	Phase III
Power	Meaningful Work	Supportive Relationship	Fulfillment of the Dream
Identification	Idealization	Self-assertion	Internalization

undisturbed. This conclusion supports the findings of Phillips (1977) noted in Chapter One.

In contrast, the mentor is a person who shares "the dream"—not necessarily a consciously formulated career goal, but rather a cherished perception of self (ego ideal). While the mentor can also be a sponsor, one who promotes, this need not be the case. The mentor may promote the protégé by association and influence, yet he may not be the person who literally promotes the protégé in the job situation. Even when the mentor and protégé are in the same company, the act of promoting from one job to another is an administrative function. The act of preparing a protégé for promotion is a teaching function. Clearly, the latter function is of a higher order.

In reviewing all of the interviews both of the mentor and so-called non-mentor group, one thing stands out: The emotional involvement in a *true* mentoring relationship goes far beyond the utility of the relationship in terms of sponsorship or career modeling. As described in detail in Chapters Four and Five, a caring develops which makes the relationship at once stronger in every respect and at the same time much more tenuous. Each partner in such a relationship invests so much of self that each becomes the more vulnerable to the other.

The willingness to be vulnerable to the other person is the key to the issue of trust, which in turn is the key to the development of a true mentoring relationship. The fundamental distinction, then, is essentially one of emotional involvement (ego) or the lack of it.

The degree of emotional intensity expressed by the protégés during the interviews when talking of their mentors was dramatic, revealing and strikingly different from their demeanor when discussing sponsors or other role models. The visible physical changes noted are much the same as those associated with people talking about a loved one. The eyes begin to sparkle, the muscles around the lips soften, the tone of voice becomes vibrant, the breathing accelerates, a tremendous feeling of excitement is communicated; the words used are words of love, *not* utility. It is an unmistakable phenomenon.

Needless to say, should one lose a mentor through misunderstanding, disenchantment or possibly death, feelings of anguish, anger or despair are predictable, as Daniel Levinson (1978) suggests.

In summary then, it can be said that sponsors are appreciated; but

CHARACTERISTIC ELEMENTS (continued)

Elements	Phase I	Phase II	Phase III
Emotional Involvement	Respect	Affection	Love

Figure 11 consolidates these distinguishing characteristics in the process of mentoring and keys them to the three phases which were identified and discussed in detail in Chapters Five, Six and Seven: namely, Initiation, Development, and Termination. Let us trace these characteristic elements through each phase of the relationship in turn.

The power of the mentor makes it possible for the protégé to receive a range of rewards which have real value for the protégé. During the Initiation Phase, the reward is meaningful work to do—work which is challenging and growth-facilitating. In the Development Phase, the power of the mentor in terms of status and influence provides the protégé with referent power and a supportive relationship which heightens her self-esteem. And by the Termination Phase, all of the powers of the mentor together with the evolving abilities of the protégé make it possible for the protégé to realize her potential.

The degree of identification with the mentor proceeds along familiar lines in much the same way that children identify with their parents or significant others. In the Initiation Phase, the mentor is idealized into an all-powerful, all-knowing, Godlike figure. As the protégé becomes more conscious of her own strengths, the need to test the reality of that strength is dramatized by numerous incidents of self-assertion. Mentor and protégé spar with one another and test wills. The confrontation during this period, contrived and real, is healthy and predictable. The stronger the protégé gets, the less Godlike the mentor seems. Finally, the most admired attributes of the mentor (and some of the least admired, too) are internalized and become part of the protégé's professional repertoire of behaviors.

The emotional involvement and intensity builds throughout the various stages of the relationship. In the Initiation Phase, feelings of respect, admiration, and gratitude are experienced. As the interactions between mentor and protégé increase, the protégé develops in line with the mentor's expectations. Feelings of affection develop between the pair in the context of mutual respect and admiration. In the final stage of the relationship, mentor and protégé reach an exquisite level of understanding which enables them to love one another unconditionally. They achieve the emotional maturity to accept one another as they really are: professionally distinguished, perhaps; but less than perfect human beings.

The Process of Mentoring

Let us examine once again the behaviors, perceptions, and feelings which were identified as dominant during each stage of the mentoring process—Initiation, Development, and Termination. (See pp. 37.)

As we examine the behaviors of the mentor, we find that we are looking at an activity component, task-relevant behaviors. When we examine the perceptions of the protégé, we are looking at a personality component, an individual's unique perception of the world. And when we examine the feelings of the protégé, we are looking at an emotional component, a person's visceral response to what is being experienced externally and internally.

Taken as a gestalt, these three components present a reasonably coherent picture of the dynamics of the mentoring process over time. The components are interdependent, and the process is interactive.

For example, the same behaviors given different perceptions and emotional contexts render different outcomes in the interactive process. How the behaviors of the mentor are interpreted depends upon the perceptions of the protégé, not just the functional aspects of the behaviors, but the situational context in which they occur. This interaction is further complicated by a host of subliminal signals exchanged between mentor and protégé. So while we may regard a particular behavior as having a generally constructive effect in and of itself, its real force exists in the meaning attributed to the behavior by the protégé.

We infer from our analysis of the data that while it is the mentor who initiates the process of mentoring, it is the protégé who signals the shift from one phase to the next. This could be interpreted to mean that it is the protégé who controls the progress of the relationship. It is our sense, however, that the progress of the relationship depends also upon the critical judgment of the mentor. He decides when to acknowledge the signal and when to yield to the pressure of the protégé. Readiness to move on to the next phase may be in the form of an overt signal on the part of the protégé, or it may be a subliminal signal perceived by the mentor in the protégé's demeanor. In either case, the decision to act on the signal rests with the mentor.

The mentor's judgment in the timing of this forward movement in the process of mentoring determines in large measure the success or failure of the relationship. If the mentor yields too soon, the protégé may falter and growth to potential may be jeopardized. If the mentor is reluctant to yield, the relationship may become stalled or irreparably damaged. His actions must reflect an accurate assessment of the emotional needs of the protégé as well as a dispassionate appraisal of her professional development at the particular moment. The mentor plays his most significant role in the process of mentoring at these critical junctures between phases.

Repeated Themes in the Behavior of Mentors

Phase I
- Recognizes protégé's ability/talent.
- Sets especially high standards of performance.
- Is extremely demanding.
- Encourages protégé (seldom verbally).

Phase II
- Teaches protégé the "tricks of the trade."
- Gives protégé all the responsibility she can handle (professional as well as personal).
- Thrusts protégé into areas for which she has no apparent expertise or experience.
- Directs and shapes through critical questioning.
- Publicizes protégé's achievements.
- Promotes steadily and often (or suggests that this be done, usually from above).
- Protects.

Phase III
- Provides opportunities to learn by osmosis, observation, and association.
- Recommends protégé to top management (usually of the parent company) or to the board of directors.
- Lets go.

Repeated Themes in the Protégé's Perception of the Mentor's Behavior

Phase I
- A sense of being molded or created by the mentor (Pygmalion syndrome).
- The pursuit of excellence as a shared value and an intrinsic reward.
- An atmosphere of expectations where demands are seen as opportunities.
- Self-concept confirmed by association with the mentor.

Phase II
- Opportunities to gain broader experience or to improve in a particular dimension.
- Challenged to think more clearly and creatively.
- Opinions and points of view heard and valued, even when they differ significantly from the mentor's.
- Free to make mistakes without fear.
- Progress based upon professional performance.

Phase III
- Awareness of one's own special strengths and contributions to the relationship.
- Fallibility of the mentor recognized.

Repeated Themes in the Protégé's Emotional Response (Feelings)

Phase I
- Gratitude, admiration and respect.
- Excitation by the association with power and its implications.
- A feeling of being somehow "special," worthy of attention, valued.

Phase II
- Feelings aroused in Phase I reinforced.
- Feeling secure and/or supported.
- Feelings of isolation.
- Feelings of resentment.

Phase III
- Pride in achievement.
- Infinite closeness.

RELEVANT THEORIES AND PRINCIPLES

First, let me suggest that it might be a useful tool to analyze organizational life in terms of its similarity to family life. This analogy is very powerful when one considers that those who reach the top of the management hierarchy—the women in this study as well as their male counterparts, the chief executive officers of the Fortune 500—spend some 20 to 25 years of their adult lives in a single organizational environment. This is longer than most children today spend with their biological families!

Harry Levinson (1962) and his colleagues at the Menninger Foundation found support for this concept in their intensive study of a large utility company. Levinson hypothesizes that "one of the significant differences between those who become executives and those who do not lies in the presence or absence of certain kinds of identification models." In much the same way that children grow and mature through identification with authority figures such as parents and teachers, a supervisor or junior executive will grow in stature and competence to the extent that superiors provide models with which he or she can identify.

The behaviors of the mentor, then, in providing for the needs of the organizational neophyte—what Harry Levinson has referred to as providing for the "ministration, maturation, and mastery needs of subordinates"—may be considered analogous to the behaviors of responsible and loving parents.

In his recent book, *The Ecology of Human Development,* sociologist Urie Bronfenbrenner (1979) provides a striking parallel between what has been described in this chapter and in preceding chapters as the principle dimensions of the process of mentoring—power, identification, and love—and what Bronfenbrenner describes as the factors most influential in successful parenting.

After an extensive review of the literature on parenting, Bronfenbrenner concludes that three factors are paramount in the rearing of children: the two-person primary relationship (what we have termed love between mentor and protégé); the shifting balance of control between adult and child (the process of identification); and the adult's power in the external world (or the power of the mentor in the business world, as the case may be).

Bronfenbrenner argues, as we have in Chapter Five, that the "quality of the relationship is crucial: the more secure and supported the developing person feels in it, the more easily communication, learning, and growth take place." Needless to say, for young children these relationships are usually with parents, but for young men and women in organizations, these relationships could be with senior members of management.

He goes on to say that "development occurs most naturally when children observe increasingly complicated activities being done by important loved people and then do such activities jointly with the same people." Finally, Bronfenbrenner suggests that "human development is affected by the amount of power in the larger society that the adults in the relationship hold. Adults cut off from power over the economic and political institutions which shape their lives," he says, "are less likely to provide the time, energy and resources needed for activities with children."

The issues that Bronfenbrenner raises—the quality of the relationship, the balance of control between the pair, and the power to reward in a meaningful way—are exactly the same issues to which our analysis of the successful mentoring relationships in this study has led us. They were described in Chapter Four and developed in Chapter Five as the crucial elements in the development and maintenance of successful mentoring relationships.

If we follow through with this analogy, we can see that certain elements of the process of mentoring are already familiar to us. In the case of children, the first four years of life have a lasting impact; so it is for the career lives of men and women in organizations.

As noted earlier, the Berlew and Hall (1966) study emphasizes the tremendous impact of encounters during the early years of organizational life, particularly the first year. Similarly, Edgar Schein (1965) emphasizes the importance of developing a "creative individualism" in dealing with the pressure toward conformity in the organizational socialization process if one seeks upward mobility. And finally, Daniel Levinson (1978) points out the problems of individuation that can occur in mid-life if these developmental needs are not met. On an organizational level, Harry Levinson (1968) points out the problems of succession which can occur if these developmental needs of junior managers are not met.

To be sure, the mentor/protégé relationship is unique, powerful, and complex, but it seems clear that it builds upon some of these well-known elements. The architecture of the relationship, however, depends upon the personalities of the participants and the setting.

Let us look again at the world as seen through the eyes of the women in the mentor and non-mentor group. Were they simply operating in different environments? Or were they experiencing the environments differently?

There is an old saying that goes: What we see is largely what we look for. In other words, what one sees is one's unique perception of the world, not necessarily a reflection of objective reality. While our outlook may be altered from time to time by our experiences, by and large, our perceptual perspective is set at a relatively early age and is something we bring to the organizational setting.

Therefore, a person with the traits characteristic of the mentor group entering an organization—a person who considers environments generally open, benign, even supportive—is likely to find it so. Conversely, a person like those in the non-mentor group, who see environments as initially frightening, even hostile, is likely to find it so. The outcome is a perceptual matter.

This is not to suggest that some environments do not contain hostile elements. Of course, they do. What it does suggest, however, is that one's perception of the world will influence one's behavior in a given environment, and that behavior will influence how one is perceived by others in that environment.

We had a clear sense of such a perceptual and behavioral difference between the mentor and non-mentor group. But it was only our sense, our perception, if you will. There is not sufficient data in this study to support such a conclusion. We have no way of knowing whether these differences are personality differences or whether they result from differing organizational contexts, or both. We do know, based on our findings, that they are important variables that can make a difference in the outcome, and they would bear closer examination in future research efforts.

To underscore the importance of these variables, let us consider two principles, one relating to organizational environments and one relating to interpersonal dynamics, which can alter the course of a mentoring relationship.

The successful mentor/protégé relationships described in Chapter Four seem to have developed in organizational environments which adhere closely to a principle of supportive relationships which was enunciated by Rensis Likert (1961) some years ago as a desirable ideal to work toward.

He said it was important that:

The leadership and other processes of the organization must be such as to insure the maximum probability that in all interactions and relationships with the organization, each member, given his/her background, values and expectations will view the experience as supportive and one which builds and maintains a sense of personal worth.

It appears from our analysis in Chapter Four that this is indeed the way in which the mentor group saw the organizational community to which they belonged. They experienced the environment as supportive in the sense that Likert describes.

Their relationships with their mentors seem to have followed yet another principle, Carl Rogers' (1961) concept of "congruence." Rogers defines congruence as "an accurate matching of experience, awareness, and communication."

Rather than attempt to paraphrase this complex construct, let us simply state the principle:

> The greater the congruence of experience, awareness, and communication on the part of one individual, the more the ensuing relationship will involve: a tendency toward reciprocal communication with a quality of increasing congruence; a tendency toward more mutually accurate understanding of the communication; improved psychological adjustments and functioning in both parties; mutual satisfaction in the relationship.
>
> Conversely, the greater the communicated incongruence of experience and awareness, the more the ensuing relationship will involve: further communication with the same quality; disintegration of accurate understanding; less adequate psychological adjustment and functioning in both parties; and mutual dissatisfaction in the relationship.

Rogers goes on to say that it is the perception of the receiver of the communication which is crucial.

From the foregoing, it seems clear that from beginning to end, each of the mentor group was engaged in a mentoring relationship which hit all of the targets cited for achieving the greatest probability of success in a growth-facilitating relationship. While true mentoring relationships are unique, complex and relatively rare in the organizational context, there is impressive evidence supporting the view that this ideal can be approximated if not fully reached at all levels of the organization.

… # chapter eleven

What to do 'til the mentor comes

> Life is either a daring adventure or nothing at all.
> HELEN KELLER

It is customary for women in our society to be self-effacing—to suggest that it was sheer luck or forces beyond themselves that catapulted them into success. In fact, all the women in this study credited their mentors and a measure of luck for their success. But their career histories suggest otherwise. A mentor may be a *necessary* but certainly not a sufficient condition to ensure career success. Moreover, what is termed "luck" may merely be a readiness to perceive opportunity.

These are not women who were sitting patiently at their desks waiting to be "discovered." If they had been, they would still be waiting! Whether consciously or unconsciously, they were actively pursuing their own dreams. Perhaps they were not following a conscious career strategy, but their behavior suggests a pathway to success which is here recommended to you.

1. Identify with Winners.
2. Work Smarter Not Harder.
3. Develop a Top Management Perspective.
4. Build Contact Credits by Sharing Information.
5. Don't Hide Your Light Under a Bushel.
6. Be Willing to Take Risks.
7. Maintain Your Identity and Integrity.
8. Use Everything You've Got, and Get What You Haven't Got.
9. Collaborate with Colleagues; Compete with Yourself.
10. Go For It!

10 STEPS TO CAREER SUCCESS

Identify with Winners

If you really want to be a winner, to be a success (success defined here in your own personal value terms), then it makes sense to seek out people who are winners. Study them. Get to know them. Learn from them. Perhaps their experience can be of value to you. Learn to associate mentally with the kind of person you would like to become. What kinds of educational and economic backgrounds do your role models have? Do they have personality characteristics in common? Do they have professional skills in common? What motivates them? What makes them tick?

Fortunately, there is a good deal of data both in this book (Chapters Three and Four) and in other sources which can give you specific professional profiles. This may help you to identify the characteristics of the milieu to which you aspire. Recall that the women in this study came from a wide range of economic backgrounds. They were well educated, and their graduate majors were job-related. Did they have personality characteristics in common? You bet they did. They all shared a very strong sense of self—a self-confidence and self-reliance that was instilled in these women early in their lives.

While one cannot go back and reorder one's childhood, one can begin at any point in life to identify with role models who exhibit qualities and traits one admires and wishes to emulate. Identification with role models is one of the most powerful growth facilitators and behavior modifiers.

As for professional skills, there is a plethora of literature which explores the characteristics of successful leaders. While there is no one success profile which researchers have been able to agree upon, they have succeeded in isolating a few key personality characteristics and a few key skills that most have in common:

- A strong ego.
- A high level of energy.
- A high level of intelligence (not to be confused with genius).
- The ability to conceptualize ideas—their own and those of others.
- The ability to make decisions based on limited or incomplete data.
- The ability to communicate well—to write succinctly and verbalize clearly.
- The ability to relate to others in a congruent fashion.

There is *nothing* more valuable to an aspiring management person than to associate with or work for someone who possesses these characteristics and skills.

What motivates them? What makes them tick? Needless to say, a generalized answer to such questions is almost impossible. We can say, however, that the women in this study were motivated in part by an internal desire to do and be the best of which they were capable.

Work Smarter Not Harder

Have you ever watched a great dancer perform—Rudolph Nureyev, Margot Fontaine, or perhaps Fred Astaire? It's always such a joy, and a bit of a mystery, too, because their artistry seems so effortless. They have all mastered one of the fundamentals of professionalism—learning to work smarter not harder. They work hard at their craft, harder than most, but they work hard to simplify, to perfect what they are doing to the point where all extraneous movements are eliminated. All their energies are focused; no movement is wasted. Each movement has been stripped to its essence until the routine is clean, precise, truly elegant. Hard work has been transformed into artistry.

Perhaps you haven't thought about what you do in those terms. Perhaps you should. Ask yourself: What can I do to make or do this better? Faster? Easier? These are not mutually exclusive conditions. If you focus your attention on improving your performance, you may be surprised to discover that superior performance can also be faster, simpler, and a lot more fun.

Another important question to ask yourself: Who do I know or where have I seen or heard of someone who does what I do better than I am presently able to do it? Seek that person out. Solicit his or her advice and help—that is, of course, if your're serious about improving your performance and not just playing a head game with yourself. Consider what you would do if you wanted to improve your tennis game. You've got it! See a pro and try to find better partners.

Unless you continue to take instructions from a tennis pro or play with partners who are superior players (preferably both), your game will not improve significantly. No matter how long you play at the game you will continue to be a marginal player. Repetition alone never improves performance. On the other hand, repetition together with professional direction, example, and reinforcement can do much to improve performance.

The management game is much the same. There are those often referred to as managers who "play" at managing and then there are those who are professional managers. The professional manager works hard to improve the routine (repertoire of skills) so that it can be reduced to its essentials. The time and energy thus released can then be used to learn new and more challenging routines. Each successive challenge reinforces one's confidence in one's own ability, and in fact, enhances one's potential. And so, the ritual of working smarter repeats itself over and over and over again.

Develop a Top Management Perspective

Developing a top management perspective sounds good, but how does one do that? And why is it important? A top management perspective is developed by establishing rapport with resource and reference people (models, if you will) at the level to which you aspire. Some of these people may be in your company, some may not. Some may even be in another industry or profession. The key thing, however, is that these resource people have expertise, knowledge and information that you do not have. Moreover, they are achievers, people at the top (or close to the top) of their respective professions.

To answer straight away: The acquisition of a top management perspective is not accomplished easily or overnight. Through repeated interaction with such people one is exposed to their culture. One gains a sense of their values: that is, what's important, what is not. What are the priorities? How does one behave in such an environment? One learns by observation, by emulation and even by osmosis. The one thing that is certain is that without exposure to top management people it is difficult, if not impossible, to gain a top management perspective.

When people are being singled out for promotion in an organization (given a track record on the existing level), the most important distinguishing characteristic is a top management perspective. Does this person see the big picture? Can he or she differentiate between strategic and operational issues? And a more universal question: Will this person fit in?

"But I don't know such people. I have no access to them," you say. Open your eyes and use the resources available to you. Supportive relationships are all around you.

Achievers want to be associated with people who are doing exciting and interesting things. If what you're doing or what you propose doing has merit and value, there will be people around who will want to give you a hand. If nothing else, they will offer you the benefit of their experience, which can be a powerful advantage.

Build Contact Credits by Sharing Information

Some people get a piece of information and hoard it, or worse yet, ignore it. Others get a piece of information and share it. Clearly, the latter are richer for having shared the information. *Information is the currency of organizational life.* Perhaps a few examples will help to illuminate this point.

One of the easiest ways of building contact credits is to be sensitive to the projects and special interests of colleagues and supervisors. Perhaps you see an article in the *Harvard Business Review* about strategic planning.

Your supervisor has just been appointed to the strategic planning committee. You send it along with a short note: "Thought this would interest you." Guess what? You have just banked a contact credit!

A colleague is going to make a marketing presentation to the steering committee this afternoon on a new software line. You read in the morning *Wall Street Journal* that your company's major competitor has just announced their campaign on a similar project. You call your colleague immediately to alert him or her to this piece of information. Your colleague may or may not have seen the announcement. It doesn't matter. Either way, you have just banked a contact credit.

You love thumbing through the want ads looking for antique bargains. Your eye lights on an ad, "Rare Victorian piano of solid rosewood in working condition." You have no need for a Victorian piano, but suddenly you remember hearing that the president just bought a Victorian home which he is restoring, and he plays the piano. That's right! You call his office on the chance that this ad may be just the lead he is looking for. It may be, it may not be. But you can be sure your thoughtful gesture will be remembered and appreciated. You have just banked another contact credit.

Some people are hesitant about sharing internally relevant information because they fear their colleagues could also use the information to advance or enhance their careers. Such fears are usually unfounded. The fact is that when you give the same information to a half dozen people, there are likely to be a half dozen *different* interpretations of the data. More importantly, few if any will be motivated to act on it. The likelihood is that those who get an idea and want to move with it are likely to call upon you for your cooperation. Remember, a piece of information can spark an idea, but an idea is only an abstraction until it is implemented.

Building contact credits is like money in the bank; you get it back with interest!

Don't Hide Your Light Under a Bushel

Women have been socialized to believe that it is somehow unladylike to call attention to oneself or to one's achievements in any overt way. One must wait to be noticed, to be recognized, to be asked.

They seem to believe that if they are "good little girls" and do what they are told and perform exceptionally well, they will be recognized and rewarded. Well, that's a nice fairy tale that has little to do with the realities of organizational life. Their value may, in fact, be recognized by their superior. He may pat them on the head, tell them what a terrific job they're doing, and even that he couldn't imagine what he would do without them. Yes indeed. But will this recognition result in a raise or a promotion? Chances are it will not *unless* they demonstrate by their manner that they are ready and that a promotion and/or a raise are realistic expectations.

People in positions of power need to be made aware of one's capabilities and experience. How are they to know that a diamond in the rough is buried in the research library? Too often women rely on their supervisor to recommend them. This is certainly a good recommendation to have, but often unreliable. A supervisor may be inclined to hold on to a good thing out of need, or may be reluctant to recommend someone with potential out of fear or envy.

One might also expect that personnel offices would review the credentials of company employees before looking outside to fill an opening, or that there is a system of internal review. There usually is a system of internal review, but it is often used as a cover after a selection is made. Most selections are made on the basis of verbal recommendations. And verbal recommendations are made on the basis of contact experience with the person or on the basis of second party opinions of one's background and capabilities.

People in decision-making positions of power must see you. They must hear about your good works, from you and from others. Even activities unrelated to your specific task ought to be shared.

Suppose you have been working for the past several years as a volunteer service director for the Office for Senior Citizens in your community. The program you have introduced there has earned national recognition. Suppose also that your company is planning to formalize its social responsibility concerns by opening a Department of Community Affairs, and they will be needing a director. You wouldn't even get a crack at this opportunity unless people in decision-making positions of power knew of your involvement and your special expertise.

Do not depend upon others to do your spade work for you. Learn to toot your own horn. This can be accomplished simply and effectively without earning you a reputation as a braggart. In your everyday discourse remember to communicate your achievements, aspirations and goals. Show interest and take pleasure in the achievements of others. Such activity is rewarding and comes under the category of intelligent self-interest. Remember, it's your career; and *no one* is more interested in it or has more to gain from your advancement than you do.

Be Willing to Take Risks

You're familiar with the old cliche, "Nothing ventured, nothing gained"? It has become a cliche because its truth is continually confirmed by experience. People who succeed—and those who want to succeed—are willing to take risks. They venture their time, their energies, and their reputations, and they risk the stigma of failure on the assumption that they've got what it takes to "make it."

Women are often reluctant to strike out on a new or untried venture. Some are even hesitant about accepting responsibility for directing activities for which they have experience and skills. They are plagued with doubt and fears of failure or somehow "looking foolish." They want to be absolutely certain they have all the answers and that success is guaranteed. Well, there is no such thing! Nobody has all the answers, and nothing is guaranteed. There are only questions to be answered and opportunities to be explored.

We pointed out earlier that visibility is essential if one's capabilities are to be recognized. Yet it is also true that with greater visibility comes greater vulnerability. And therein lies the rub. The risk involved would be minimized considerably if women were convinced of the fact that *everyone* makes mistakes. You are *expected* to make mistakes. You are just not expected to repeat the same mistakes.

The more important issue is: What does a person do when a mistake is made? How is it handled? Does the person recognize the error quickly and move adroitly to correct it? Or having acknowledged the error, does the person seek whatever help is needed?

Is the person flustered, paralyzed, or worse yet, does the person shunt responsibility onto co-workers only to repeat the same error again?

The strategy employed in either case is the difference between winners and losers. It is this behavioral difference that is observed and logged mentally by supervisors and co-workers alike. It is upon such behavioral differences that careers are built. Without the willingness to take small risks where the consequences of error are reversible and where only your ego is really at risk, you will never gain the confidence needed to take on assignments where you know in advance that your job and your reputation are on the line.

It is significant that the successful women in this study were often the first to hold a newly created position where there were no guidelines except those which they would create themselves. In yet other instances, they were the first women to hold a position formerly reserved "for men only" where the risk was not only in tackling the challenges of a new job per se, but in making one's way through a social mine field and living to tell about it.

These are women who took the risks, learned the lessons, and gained the confidence and respect of their colleagues and supervisors because they were smart and they were game.

Maintain Your Identity and Integrity

There is a popular notion that one succeeds by riding the coattails of a sponsor or mentor. Such a strategy is seriously flawed. Should the mentor or sponsor fall out of favor or leave, you have lost your vehicle and more importantly, your identity card.

One's professional identity needs to be built upon the quality of one's own performance. This is not to say that sponsors and mentors do not contribute to and enhance one's performance and potential. They do. The process needs to be one of personal growth and development of *your* unique potential, *your* identity. You must gain credibility in your own right.

Similarly, one must maintain one's integrity. It's not fashionable somehow to talk about integrity in organizational life today. Corporate "politics" is the operative buzz word. Yet personal integrity is an organizational value and always commands respect. Preserving one's integrity in a competitive and political environment is not an easy matter, but it is possible if you learn to focus on issues rather than personalities. As the balance of power shifts in an organization, one maintains integrity by the consistency of one's response to issues.

The person in a position of power wants all the allies he can get. So if you happen to be on his side of an issue, that's a definite plus. On the other hand, if you have established a reputation as a person of integrity, the fact that you do not back "his issue" will not hurt you. It is understood that it is the *issue* you oppose, not the person. You will have developed a reputation, an "identity," built on your performance and your integrity as a person.

Use Everything You've Got, and Get What You Haven't Got

Use everything you've got and get what you need, whether it's education, experience, organizational strategy—whatever. Too often we limit ourselves and allow ourselves to be limited by arbitrary criteria which have little if anything to do with the actual doing of a job.

For example, a company may be advertising for a Director of Publications. They stipulate: "master's in journalism." What they really want is someone who edits well, conceptualizes well, is creative and knows how to organize the work of creative people. A person with these capabilities but without the degree credentials will be hard pressed even to get an interview—much less the job.

What's a person to do? If it's an opportunity you really want, you'll use every personal contact you have to get an audience—an opportunity to show what you can do. It becomes the responsibility of the person who wants to get ahead, therefore, to make the match between what is actually needed and what he or she, as an individual, has to offer to fill that need.

There is yet another scenario that is all too familiar. How many women do you know who feel handicapped in today's MBA-oriented business world because they majored in Early Childhood Education or something more esoteric, perhaps Greek philosophy? Are they effectively closed out of consideration for advancement in the business community? They don't have to be if they are resourceful and examine their strengths in relation to opportunities.

For example, an elementary school teacher might not immediately think of a career in the computer industry as an alternative possibility, but there is a potential match there. Consider the fact that one of the key strengths of elementary school teachers is the ability to communicate strategic pieces of information sequentially in bite-sized installments. Each piece can be understood more easily by the children and then integrated into more complex concepts to be learned later. This skill is precisely the same one used by management trainers in the computer industry to educate buyers and users of software packages. While the students in this case are not children, they are nevertheless managers unsophisticated in computer technology. Certainly the content of a management seminar differs from the everyday third-grade curriculum, but the skill required in organizing and communicating the material is the same.

The teacher in this example is a professional with a marketable skill. What is lacking is a knowledge of computers, something which can be picked up at any college or university in a relatively short period of time. Remember: use everything you've got, *and get what you haven't got.* No need to feel handicapped or discouraged because you don't have an MBA. What you *do* need is to be prepared to invest time and energy in acquiring whatever additional educational backup may be needed to make a potential career opportunity a reality.

Collaborate with Colleagues; Compete with Yourself

Women are often accused of not being "team players." It has even been suggested by some authors that their organizational potential has been somehow jeopardized because they didn't engage in contact sports as little girls. Presumably little boys learn how to be team players on the football field. Perhaps. The important issue is not whether or not one played football, but whether or not one learned to work in harmony with others, balancing strengths and weaknesses. People who are successful in organizational life are people who know how to work in harmony with others.

Facility for collaborative effort can be learned in any number of ways. A couple of examples will underscore the point. Did you ever play an instrument in the school band? Did you ever sing in a chorus or church choir? Have you ever participated in a school play or musical? Of course you have. We all have at one time or another. In each of these activities, the success of the program depends upon the collaboration of group members. They have to know their own parts and the parts of their colleagues, so if someone goofs, someone else can cover. Then, there is the issue of timing. One cannot go off tooting on one's own, because the objective is *harmony.* So one must learn to pace oneself, and keep an eye on the director.

Does teamwork or collaboration mean one is forever in lockstep with one's colleagues? Certainly not. To push our analogy a little further, consider the member of a choir who is also a soloist. Here the objective is not just harmony, but individuality as well. As soloist, one is free to interpret the music, change the pace, experiment with variation in tone; in short, to do his or her own thing.

As for the much-maligned notion of competition, it can be a positive force if properly directed. Learn to compete against your own best effort or a standard to which you aspire. Do not waste time and energy competing against your colleagues. Zero-sum games are counterproductive in the long run. Use that energy to pursue excellence in yourself—to improve your own individual performance. You will become a much more valuable team member while practicing to become an organizational "star."

Go For It!

If vague aspirations are to become realities, one must take the initiative by:

1. Deciding what it is you want to do—the direction in which you want to go.
2. Developing an operational plan to get you there.
3. Following through on the plan.

Remember, people who succeed (defined in terms of your own value system) have the *will to succeed*. Do not burden your brain with the thought that if you don't have a mentor or a sponsor your chance for advancement is diminished. Go for it—whatever "it" is. What is the worst that could happen? You will have given it your best shot and failed. But you will have been a "contender."

One of the most poignant scenes in the movie *On the Waterfront* takes place between a simple-minded prizefighter, played by Marlon Brando, and his brother, a member of the underworld that controls the fight game. The scene takes place in a cab. The older brother is pressing money into the youthful Brando's hand for having thrown an important fight. Mumbling in an agonized way, Brando expresses his deep dissatisfaction with having had to hold back, to have reined in his desire to win and to have "taken a fall." The older brother assures him that holding back and taking the "sure money" was better than getting his brains knocked out "for nothing."

Simple-minded though the prizefighter is, he is not so simple that he does not understand he has lost a valuable opportunity. Grasping his brother's lapels, Brando cries, "But you don't understand. I could have been a *contender*. I could have been *somebody!*"

By giving each opportunity your best effort, by developing some of the foregoing behavioral attitudes, you will have blossomed into the kind of person whose real potential is more easily identified by a mentor. You will have become a "contender."

Bibliography

Becker, Howard, and Anselm Strauss, "Careers, Personality and Adult Socialization," *American Journal of Sociology* 62 (1956): 253-63.

Berlew, D., and Hall, D, "The Socialization of Managers: Effects of Expectation on Performance," *Administrative Science Quarterly* 11 (September 1966): 207-23.

Bernard, Jessie, *Academic Women*. University Park: Pennsylvania State University Press, 1964.

Bronfenbrenner, Urie, *The Ecology of Human Development: Experiments by Nature and Design*. Cambridge, Mass.: Harvard University Press, 1979.

Business Week, November 24, 1975, p. 58. "Up the Ladder, Finally."

Cussler, Margaret, *The Woman Executive*. New York: Harcourt Brace, 1958.

Epstein, Cynthia, *Woman's Place*. Berkeley: University of California Press, 1970.

Etzioni, Amatai, *A Comparative Analysis of Complex Organizations*. New York: Free Press, 1961.

Goffman, Erving, *Stigma: Notes on the Management of Spoiled Identity*. Englewood Cliffs, N.J.: Prentice-Hall, 1963.

Hall, Oswald, "The Stages of a Medical Career," *American Journal of Sociology* 53 (1948): 327-36.

Hennig, Margaret and Jardim, Anne, *The Managerial Woman*. Garden City: Anchor Press/Doubleday, 1977.

Homans, George C., *The Human Group*. New York: Harcourt Brace, 1950.

Kanter, Rosabeth Moss, *Men and Women of the Corporation*. New York: Basic Books, 1977.

Levinson, Daniel J., *The Seasons of a Man's Life*. New York: Alfred A. Knopf, Inc., 1978.

Levinson, Harry, *The Exceptional Executive*. Cambridge, Mass.: Harvard University Press, 1968.

Levinson, H., C. Price, K. Munden, H. Mandl, and S. Solley, *Men, Management, and Mental Health*. Cambridge, Mass.: Harvard University Press, 1962.

Likert, Rensis, *New Patterns of Management*. New York: McGraw-Hill, 1961.

Livingstone, Sterling J., "Pygmalion in Management," *Harvard Business Review*, "How to Handle Executive People," 12 studies.

McClelland, David C., *The Achieving Society*. Princeton: D. Van Nostrand Co., 1961.

Phillips, Linda Lee, "Mentors and Protégés: A Study of the Career Development of Women Managers and Executives in Business and Industry." Ph.D. Dissertation, UCLA, School of Education, 1977.

Roche, Gerald R., "Much Ado About Mentors," *Harvard Business Review* 57 (1979): 14-28.

Rogers, Carl R., *On Becoming a Person*. Boston: Houghton Mifflin Company, 1961. See also "The Characteristics of a Helping Relationship," *Personnel and Guidance Journal* 37 (1958): 6-16.

Schein, Edgar H., "Organizational Socialization and the Profession of Management." (From the third Douglas M. McGregor Memorial Lecture of the Alfred P. Sloan School of Management, Massachusetts Institute of Technology.) See also: *Organizational Psychology*. Englewood Cliffs: Prentice-Hall, 1965.

Shapiro, E., F. Haseltine, and M. Rowe, "Moving Up: Role Models, Mentors, and The 'Patron System,' " *Sloane Management Review* 19 (1978): 51-58.

Sheehy, Gail, *Passages*. New York: Bantam, 1976.

Zaleznik, Abraham, "Managers and Leaders: Are They Different?" *Harvard Business Review* 55 (1978).

SUPPLEMENTARY BIBLIOGRAPHY

Berry, Dick, "As Women Move into Management," *Management* 29 (1977): 10-13.

Bolton, Elizabeth B., Luther Humphreys, and R. Wade, "A Training Model for Women—An Androgynous Approach," *Personnel Journal* 56 (1977): 230-34.

Ekberg-Jordan, Sandra, "Preparing for the Future—Commitment and Action," *Atlanta Economic Review* 26 (1976).

Gackenback, Jayne I., Marian Burke, et al., "Women in Business Seminar—Exploring an Approach to Change in Sex Role Awareness," *Atlantic Review* 26 (1976).

Loring, R., and R. Wells, *Breakthrough: Women in Management*. New York: Van Nostrand Reinhold, 1972.

McCloy, R.L., "Developing Women in Business," *Industrial Management* 18 (1976): 13-19.

Orth, Charles D., and Rederick Jacobs, "Women in Management: Pattern for Change," *Harvard Business Review* (July-August 1970).

Rosen, Benson, and Jerdee, "On the Job Sex Bias—Increasing Managerial Awareness," *The Personnel Administrator* 22 (1977): 15-18.

Schein, Virginia Ellen, "The Relationship Between Sex Role Stereotypes and Requisite Management Characteristics," *Journal of Applied Psychology* 57 (1973): 95-100.

Thompson, Jacqueline, "Patrons, Rabbis, Mentors—Whatever You Call Them, Women Need Them Too." *MBA Magazine*, February 1975, pp. 26-35.

Index

A

Affirmative Action, 25-26
　correlation of with age of women, 26
　table, 25
Affluent Society, The, 9

B

Becker and Strauss, work of, 3

C

Cantor, Eddie, quoted, 33
Collaboration with others, 107-8
　distinguished from lockstep condition, 108
　learning of, 107
　women, problems of, 107
Competition, 108

D

Development phase of mentoring relationship:
　behavioral themes of mentors, 50-53
　　experiences, 51-52
　　feelings of mentors, 53
　　table, 51
　　teaching, 52
　demands vs. freedom, 59
　protégés feelings in, 56-58
　　depth, 57
　　experiences, 57
　　social isolation, 57-58
　　support, 57
　　table, 56
　　"woman's wage," problem of, 58
　protégés' perceptions of mentors behavior, 53-56
　　arrival, feelings of, 55
　　assignment challenges, 54
　　experiences, 54, 55-56
　　table, 54
Djilas, Milovan, quoted, 21

E

Ecology of Human Devlopment, The, 93
Effort, rationalizing of, 99-100
　dancers, example of, 99
　management as game, 100

Effort *(cont.)*
  questions to ask self, 100
Egerton, 3
Epstein, 6
Exceptional Executive, The, 5
Executives, male, compared to women, 28-30
  parallels, 29
  pay, 29
  prevalence of mentoring in, 29
  quality of relationship, 29-30
Expectations, as factor in performance, 47-48
  Berlew and Hall, work of on, 48
  initial behaviors of mentor, 48
  reasons to encourage, 48

G

Galbraith, John Kenneth, 9
Goethe, quoted, 1
Goffman, 3

H

Half, Robert, quoted, 39
Hall, 3
Heidrick and Struggles, survey by, 3-4
Hennig, 7
Huxley, Aldous, quoted, 50

I

Identity and integrity, maintenance, of, 105-6
  allies of powerful people, 105-6
  integrity, problem of, 105
  professional identity, 105
"In" group, entry to, 2-3
  Jewel Companies, experience of, 3
  membership in, value of, 3
  mentor system, advantages of, 2
  norms in, 3
  "Young Turks," opinions of, 2
Information, sharing of, 101-2
  contact credits, concept, 101, 102
  marketing presentation, example, 101
  piano, example, 101
  reluctance to share, 101
Initiation phase, of mentoring relationship:
  mentors, behavior of in, 40-42
    demands of, 41-42
    initiation, 40
    and talent, recognition of, 40-41
  protégés, repeated themes in feelings of, 44-47
    association with powerful, 46
    challenge and ability, 47
    halo effect, 46
    initiation, 45
    specialness, feeling of, 45-46
  protégés, perception of mentors' behavior, 42-44
    entry into "men's work," 43
    initiation, 42-43
    standards, 43-44
Integrity. *See* Identity and integrity, maintenance of

K

Keller, Helen, 97

L

Letting go, in mentor relationship, 71-72
  analog to birth, 71
Levinson, Daniel J., work of, 4-5
Levinson, Harry, 5
Love, discussion of, 80-81
  agapē, 81
  Christ, attitudes of, 81
  eros, 81
  link to sex in West, 80
  philia, 81
  Plato, quoted on, 81
  Platonic concept, 80
  Western concept, 80, 81
Love, relationship of in mentoring, 69-71
  conflicts, 70
  development of, 70
  existential choice, 71
  Levinson, Daniel, quoted on, 70
  manipulation, avoidance of, 71
  Rogers, Carl, quoted on, 70, 71
  trust, 70
Lunding, Frank, 3

M

Maugham, Somerset, quoted, 73
Men, mentoring of, 3-6

advantages, 4-5
and career satisfaction, 4
course of relationship, 5
father/friend mixture, 4
friend type, 6
godfather type, 6
as role model, 4-5
sponsor type, 6
Mentor:
  continuum of type, 86
  discussion of by protégés, 87
  nature of, 86
  in *Odyssey*, 86
Mentor/protégé relations, phases in, 37-38
  development, 38
  establishment, 37
  termination, 38
Mentoring, nature of in women, 11-20
  Business Week criteria, 12
  defined for study, 12
  interviews in depth, 16-18
    followup questions, 17-18
    mentor, questions about, 17
    nature, 16
  mail surveys, 12-14
    age differences, mentor/protégé, 13
    education levels, 12
    goals, age at commitment to, 13
    interview choice, 13
  research questions, 11-12
  strategy and responses to interview, 18-20
    rapport, 18
    sampling, 18
  survey responses, 14-15
    executive's departure from firm, men compared to women, 15
    problems with, 14, 15
    table, 14
Mentoring, process of, 90-92
  behavior, repeated themes in, 91
  as gestalt, 90
  interaction process, complications to, 90
  progress, mentor's judgment of, 91
  protégés' emotional responses, repeated themes in, 92
  protégés' perception of behavior, repeated themes in, 92
  signals in, 90-91
Mentoring relations, elements of, 88-90
  emotional involvement, 88
  end point, 88-90
  identification level, 88
  phases, 88-89

power, 88
rewards to protégés, 89
strength, development of by protégé, 89
Mentors, perception of by women, 39
Mentors, for top businesswomen, 26-28
  characteristics of, table, 27
  compared with survey by Phillips, 30-31
  duration of relationship, 27
  finding of, 27-28
  as former protégés, 28
  prevalence, 26-27
  summary, 31-32
Mentors, unrecognized and unacknowledged, 75-77
  denial pattern about, 77
  husband and wife team, 76-77
  outside organization, 75
  sexual involvement, 76
Mill, John Staurt, quoted, 63
Moll, Albert, work of, 1
Motivation, 48-49
  McClelland, work of, 49
  work, status of, 49

O

Organization, life of, analysis of, 92-96
  Bronfenbrenner, Urie, work of, 93
  compared to family, 92-93
  compared to parenting, 93-94
  congruence between individuals, 96
  early encounters in, effects of, 94
  Levinson, H., work of, 93
  Likert, Rensis, work of, 95-96
  perception, effects of, 95
Ortega y Gasset, José, quoted, 80

P

Pave, Irene, 11
Peers, 86
Phillips, Linda Lee, work of, 7
Protégés, female, study group profile, 33-37. *See also entries under Mentoring*
  as assistants, 36
  companies found in, 33
  compared to males, 36-37
  duration of mentoring relationships, 35, 36
  earnings, 35
  education, 34
  entry level positions, table, 35